Conflict
Management
and Organization
Development

An Expanded Edition

Conflict Management and Organization Development

An Expanded Edition

WILLEM F. G. MASTENBROEK

Holland Consulting Group,
Amsterdam, The Netherlands

JOHN WILEY & SONS
Chichester · New York · Brisbane · Toronto · Singapore

Other Wiley Editorial Offices

John Wiley & Sons, Inc., 605 Third Avenue,
New York, NY 10158-0012, USA

Jacaranda Wiley Ltd, G.P.O. Box 859, Brisbane,
Queensland 4001, Australia

John Wiley & Sons (Canada) Ltd, 22 Worcester Road,
Rexdale, Ontario M9W 1L1, Canada

John Wiley & Sons (SEA) Pte Ltd, 37 Jalan Pemimpin #05-04,
Block B, Union Industrial Building, Singapore 2057

Library of Congress Cataloging-in-Publication Data

Mastenbroek, W. F. G.
    [Conflicthantering en organisatie-ontwikkeling. English]
    Conflict management and organization development / Willem F. G.
Mastenbroek. — Expanded ed.
        p.   cm.
    "First edition 1987, expanded edition 1993"—CIP verso t.p.
    Includes bibliographical references and indexes.
    ISBN 0-471-94141-7 (pbk.)
    1. Organizational change.   2. Organizational behavior.
3. Conflict management.   I. Title.
HD58.8.M32513   1993
658.4—dc20   93–17955
                                                                 CIP

British Library Cataloguing in Publication Data

A catalogue record for this book is available from the British Library

ISBN 0-471-94141-7 (paper)

Typeset in 10/12 Times by Acorn Bookwork, Salisbury, Wiltshire
Printed and bound in Great Britain by Biddles Ltd, Guildford, Surrey

To Norbert Elias

Contents

Preface

The study to be presented here forms a bridge between the theory of organizations and the practice of professional consulting work. The 'systems model' and the 'action model' are interwoven into a single organizational theory—a network theory. In practical sense, this theoretical foundation enables consultants to perceive conflicts between parties in organizations as less threatening and sometimes as a lever towards more productivity. This makes it easier to handle them in a more relaxed manner and brings high-quality solutions within closer reach. An aspect perhaps even more important to many readers is the book's ample attention to 'cultural interventions' to make organizations more vital and more manageable.

The popularity of organization development diminished after 1975, and the no-nonsense approach to organizational consulting came into its prime. One objective of this book is to keep valuable elements in the organizational development approach from being lost and to integrate them with other strategies and methods of organizational change.

Some corporate lessons of the past five years have brought about new shifts in organizational thinking: organizational culture occupies a central position in the concepts of the 'excellent organization'. This is not primarily due to social considerations (which were dominant in organization development) but to criteria such as effectiveness, flexibility and efficiency. The intervention theory described here integrates organizational development concepts with prevailing points of emphasis in the cultural approach to organizations.

This book is the fruit of ten years of consulting work as well as of a period of teaching and research at the Free University of Amsterdam. Two editions have appeared in The Netherlands. The entirely revised 1986 edition formed the basis for this English translation. The book expresses something of the ongoing struggle which appears to be necessary to get a grasp on organizational problems. The struggle could never have led to this result without continuous professional exchange and friendly encouragement from my colleagues at the Free University and at the Holland Consulting Group in Amsterdam. Here I mention, P. A. E. van de Bunt and Dr E. van der Vliert, but I want to thank each and every one of them. In addition I am extremely grateful to Prof. E. C. H. Marx for the way in which he supported me in this work. His well-considered and encouraging ideas and remarks were always particularly stimulating. Mrs Carol Stennes translated the original Dutch version into English. Without her efforts this book could never have been published. I am very grateful to her for her endeavours to render the 'professional jargon' as perfectly as possible.

Willem Mastenbroek

Preface to Expanded Edition

Gurus come and go, the problems of organizational life remain! Competition compels organizations to mobilize their resources and to develop motivating conditions. The past five years have provided me and my colleagues with many experiences of change management, improving organizational design, and managing conflicts. The concepts described in this book have been a great help. I have condensed and focused these experiences in a new chapter—Chapter 9— 'Organizational Conditions for Competitive Advantage'. The focus is on matters of organizational design and change. The concepts and models of the first edition proved useful and were validated by many experiences. At the same time we are now able to be more specific about their application. In my opinion these findings are of great relevance. Accelerating competition and the progressive extension and condensation of dependencies within and between organizations raise problems of coordination and flexibility. If we cannot combine these increasing interdependencies with a fostering of autonomy and accountability of organizational units, the result will be increased rigidity and demotivation. A current example is the wretched situation of organizations in Eastern Europe. Closer to home, the problems faced by some large corporations, such as Philips, Dasa and General Motors, show clearly the struggle we have to wage with rigidity, demotivation and bureaucracy. Chapter 9 is of direct relevance to the crucial issues of reducing complexity and raising motivational levels in organizations. I hope it, together with the other chapters of this book, will give managers, consultants and students a sense of orientation and of inspiration.

Willem Mastenbroek

1 Intervention Theory: Goals and Outline

1.1 INTRODUCTION

The objective of the intervention theory described in this book is to present effective ways of handling a wide range of problems in organizations. In addition, this intervention theory treats strategic questions aimed at the systematic creation of successful structural and cultural conditions in organizations. Important elements of this intervention theory are: (1) organizational development interventions; (2) conflict management techniques; (3) managerial and organizational principles related to organizational success.

The major characteristics of this intervention theory are: (a) its attempt to link strong theoretical concepts and very practical recommendations; (b) its emphasis on the 'political' aspect of organizations; and (c) its unusual combination of organizational development, conflict handling and principles of organizational success.

These three characteristics deserve some elucidation, since they are central to this book:

(a) The *gap between the practice* of organizing and consulting and *the theories* about organizations and consultancy has often amazed me. Few theories about organizations offer much to go on in practice. In my experience, as well as that of many colleagues, common sense and intuition are often the best guides. Given the urgency and the importance of the problems with which consultants are concerned, the relatively low scientific level of organizational consultancy is highly unsatisfactory. It also provides a great challenge. By attempting to create a better fit between the level of specific organizational problems and practical interventions on the one hand, and the level of theories about organizations and interventions on the other, I hope to provide a firmer basis for our efforts in organizations.

(b) A second challenge is the theoretical and practical problems involved in *conflicts of interest* and *the political reality of organizations*. These problems will receive much attention in this book. At a practical level I have looked for more effective interventions and consulting skills, while trying to clarify at a theoretical level how these problems relate to other types of problems and how they all fit into an organizational theory.

(c) Third, I feel it is important to affirm the accomplishments of organizational development. Despite increasing criticism on some weak aspects of organizational development (OD), we must not neglect its positive sides. Its most important contributions must be retained and consolidated. Specifically, I have in mind *OD's process orientation: improving the way in which people in organizations work together*. The *interventions* created by organizational development are also important. This arsenal of interventions, which is constantly being expanded, tested and refined by organizational development specialists, is one of behavioural science's most important contributions to organizational consultancy. Originally oriented to the emotional aspect of relationships in small groups, these interventions have been expanded in recent years to cover a broad area of problems between people, groups and organizations. Surveys are given by French and Bell (1984) and Huse (1980). I have attempted to incorporate this arsenal of interventions in this book.

1.2   WHAT KIND OF CONSULTING

In this book we will use intervening or consulting in organizations to refer to consultancy with a social science background. Much of this consulting is called 'organizational development'. Another term we encounter is 'planned change'. Planned change is a more comprehensive term than organizational development and it better covers what is meant here by social science consultancy. Organization development is somewhat narrower because OD specialists tend to emphasize goals such as humanization, personal development, improving social relationships and developing a climate of openness and trust. This has given the term 'organizational development' somewhat idealistic connections, which is not the case with planned change. Terms such as 'organizational consultancy' or 'intervening in organizations' are frequently used in this book. Sometimes a term like 'behavioural science' is added. What these terms are intended to express can be defined as follows: 'A method of applying social knowledge and social skills in order to improve structural and cultural conditions in organizations and to solve or regulate problems between organizational units.'

1.3   STRUCTURE AND CONTENT

The link to be formed between conceptual models, practical experiences and solutions is reflected in the structure of this book. The theory–practice relationship as shown in Figure 1.1 will help clarify this. Figure 1.1 shows that the gap between theory and practice, which will receive attention in this book, can be seen in a number of ways. We can look at the distance between a general change strategy and practical interventions by consultants (link 4 in Figure

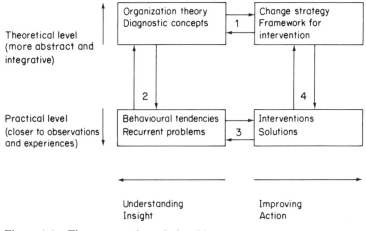

Figure 1.1   Theory–practice relationships

1.1). We can also ask how easily we can link behaviour and problems in organizations with organization theory (link 2 in the figure). Moreover, even if it is possible to place behaviour and problems in an overall theory, it still leaves us with the need for specific interventions and solutions (link 3). Then there is a gap between organization theory and change strategy. By this I mean the extent to which organization theory provides general guide-lines for improving organizations (link 1 in Figure 1.1).

In order to link consulting practice and theory more firmly, it is important to strengthen the relationships between the four elements. This will be attempted in the chapters that follow. In Chapter 2 an organization theory is described in which behavioural tendencies of people in organizations and recurrent organizational problems are easy to place. *The essence of this theory is that organizations are viewed as networks of subunits. Relations between units are characterized by a mixture of co-operation and competition. People are dependent on each other, but they also have self-interests.* In addition, this

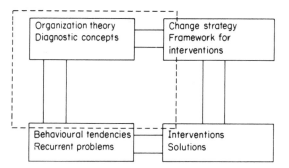

Figure 1.2   Contents of Chapter 2

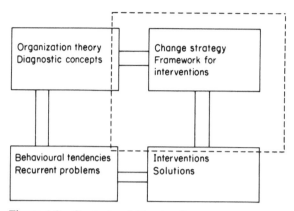

Figure 1.3   Contents of Chapter 3

chapter discusses the direction of change for organizations. The area covered by Chapter 2 is shown in Figure 1.2.

The direction of change presented in Chapter 2 is elaborated in Chapter 3 in the form of structural and cultural conditions. This chapter also explains how these conditions can be created. Direction of change and approach together form a strategy of change. Figure 1.3 shows the subject-matter of this chapter.

Chapters 2 and 3 are written from an integrative and generalizing point of view, while establishing a link to concrete problems and interventions. The more practical level is emphasized in Chapters 4, 5 and 6. Various types of problems and behavioural tendencies in organizations are discussed and interventions appropriate to them are given. Short cases describing problems and interventions are also presented. We will see how behavioural tendencies and problems fit in the categories that are fundamental to the organization theory described here. Figure 1.4 shows how the contents of these three chapters fit in the theory–practice relationship.

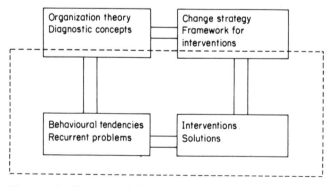

Figure 1.4   Contents of Chapters 4, 5 and 6

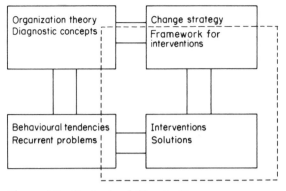

Figure 1.5   Contents of Chapter 7

Chapter 4 explores the connections between power relations, behaviour and recurrent problems. Possible interventions and solutions are also described.

Chapter 5 investigates behaviour evoked by the allocation of scarce resources and the problems faced by those involved in such situations. In this chapter, I have also tried to make the area described more accessible to interventions.

Chapter 6 takes up instrumental and social-emotional relations. Finally, Chapter 7 completes the picture. Here we attempt to integrate the problem areas and interventions into a clear framework. This chapter also outlines a consulting approach, describing additional intervention programmes in detail. Chapter 7 forms a link with the more general and integrative level; this is shown in Figure 1.5.

All in all we are covering an extensive area. I have endeavoured to present it systematically and methodically. I hope the regular and frequent use of summaries and concise diagrams will prove helpful to the reader.

1.4   A CENTRAL CONCEPT

Organizations are seen here as networks of interdependent units. Effective organizing is the skilful management of interdependencies. Our attention focuses on interdependencies or relations. There is always something peremptory and arbitrary about any choice of central concepts, especially for readers who may be accustomed to regarding other categories as fundamental. Relations are of central importance, in my opinion, because social reality is formed by the interaction between social units. Organizing and organizational consultancy always deal with the structuring and regulation of relations between units in organizations.

Moreover, it is often the problems and tensions in the relations between units in increasingly complex networks that are a great challenge to us. Keeping mutual relations effective and preventing the inevitable frictions from escalating is of primary importance.

I set great store by the diagnostic and explanatory value of the nature of relations. Problems and behavioural tendencies can often be explained by relational matters.

In matters one perceives as fundamental, further differentiation is unavoidable. As a result, I distinguish *four types of relations* which also can be seen as four aspects of a relation. These are:

1. *Power and dependency relations*. People in organizations influence to some extent the behaviour of others; usually people attempt to increase their own opportunities and capacities in this respect and to strengthen their positions with respect to others.
2. *Negotiating relations*. People in organizations must share all sorts of 'scarce resources'. In the decision-making on the allocation of these scarce resources, people are dependent on one another in order to get their own share.
3. *Instrumental relations*. People in organizations are 'means of production' for one another: they need the work of others in order to produce something themselves.
4. *Socio-emotional relations*. There are emotional ties between people in organizations. These are sometimes person-to-person in the form of affinities or antipathies, often group and organization oriented in the form of a positively or negatively charged common identity and 'we-feeling'.

This distinction is fundamental, because the four types of relations have corresponding behavioural tendencies and central problems as well as groups of interventions appropriate to them. For types 3 and 4 an extensive arsenal of interventions is available, among them Taylor's scientific management tradition and other instrumental approaches aimed at a logical division of labour, exact job descriptions, strict supervision and a well-regulated work flow. Other aspects of these approaches are planning techniques and the more behavioural science-based models of problem-solving and decision-making.

In the past explicit attention to the quality of socio-emotional relations was stimulated by the human relations approach and by organizational development. This requires a different type of intervention—for instance, the formation of cohesive work teams under participative leadership. It involves attempts to improve the social climate, to develop openness and trust in mutual relations and to fulfil the needs for personal growth. This book somewhat neglects instrumental and socio-emotional relations. Chapter 2 will show how these two types of relations fit into the theoretical framework used here. In Chapter 6 we will briefly discuss related behavioural tendencies, central problems and interventions appropriate to them. References for further reading will be given, as these areas have already been extensively explored. Because of this I felt it more important to concentrate on the less familiar areas of power, dependency and negotiating relations.

It is much less clear how we are to deal with them. Exploring and developing effective interventions is one of the objectives of this book. It will take considerable effort before we have amassed a similar wealth of interventions as is presently available in the other two areas.

1.5 SUMMARY

This book is about the management of interdependencies in organizations. An organization theory and a closely related change strategy and consulting approach are described. Much attention is devoted to concrete organizational problems and practical interventions—particularly problems related to power, dependency and negotiation.

Together these elements make up an intervention theory. The objective of this intervention theory is to help in effectively solving a wide range of organizational problems and in developing stimulating structural and cultural conditions in organizations.

2 Organization Theory: Organizations as Networks

2.1 INTRODUCTION

This chapter will explain the organization theory as it is applied in this book. Organizational sociology offers two frameworks which we want to use: the parties model and the systems model. But there are drawbacks to both of them: (1) they are too one-sided; (2) they are not easy to put into practice. This chapter is an attempt to integrate the two models. We also need an organization theory that provides a framework for interventions. *It must help in the diagnosis but it must also answer the question 'And now what?'*

The (Section 2.2) begins with a survey by Lammers of the two most important schools in organizational sociology, the system model and the parties model. This is the first step towards an integration of the two models. The section concludes with the choice of several key concepts.

In Section 2.3 the model is developed into a view of organizations as *networks of subunits between which four types of relations* can be distinguished. These four types of relations will be defined, and it will be shown how they fit into the systems model and the parties model. The interaction between the four types of relations is concisely expressed by the term '*the one-on-three model*'. Power and dependency relations are seen as the most important type, and so they will be treated separately. Next, how the four types of relations are expressed in the *structure* and the *culture* of the organization is described. Section 2.4 shows how we have incorporated *both* the competitive and the co-operative processes in organizations into one organization theory. The final-section (Section 2.5) recapitulates the most important points.

2.2 KEY CONCEPTS: ORGANIZATIONS AS NETWORKS

The systems model and the parties model are the two most common paradigms in organizational sociology. According to Lammers (1983), they are

Table 2.1   Differences between systems model and parties model

	The systems model	The parties model
1. What is the chief unit of analysis	The organization as an entity with certain functional requirements	Subgroups with self-interests
2. How durable is an organization?	Stable, with inherent forces towards self-preservation	Unstable; at best a 'community of interests'
3. What driving forces are emphasized?	A sense of norms and coherence	Sanctions and rewards
4. What image of man is presupposed?	A social being concerned with the organization's interests	A cool, calculating being concerned with self-interests
5. What is the 'emotional tone' of the analysis?	Idealistic	Cynical, realistic

two schools with fundamentally different starting-points. We encounter them under a great variety of names: for example, harmony model vs conflict model, integration vs conflict model, equilibrium vs conflict model, system vs scarce resources model, functionalistic systems vs action model.

Lammers (1983) summarized the most important differences as shown in Table 2.1.

Separately, the models are only of limited use if we are looking for a context for consultancy. They are chiefly analytical frameworks and they are handicapped by their one-sidedness. Very cautiously, Lammers pointed out a means to integration. He referred to Weber's emphasis on the *mixed* nature of organizations.

This insight, that social relations are of a mixed nature, will help us in our search for an integrative model.

Network model

In recent years the parties model has gained sway over the systems model, not least because several excellent studies of organizations used it as a basis (Baldridge, 1971; Crozier, 1964; Gouldner, 1954a,b; Pettigrew, 1973). But they did not start from the conventional form as given by Lammers. Crozier and Gouldner were particularly observant of many expressions of mutual dependency, loyalty and co-operation. The model as it was used in their studies can be summarized as follows. Organizations are *networks of interdependent groups*. The relations between these groups are characterized by co-operation *and* by competition. People are dependent on each other *and* have their own interests. In a certain sense, we might even speak of a *coalition* of divergent interests.

In organizations, individuals and groups try to strengthen their positions. People try to do so by identifying themselves with occupational groups or functional classes. People try to do so by better organizing and presenting themselves. People try to do so by making reorganizations take a course which will put them in a more central position. People try to do so by monopolizing and manipulating scarce resources which are essential to the organization. This makes an organization a *dynamic entity* of sometimes gradual, sometimes more sudden, shifts in the relations between the groups of which it is composed.*

This model needs to be worked out so that it is easier to use in organizational consulting work. The studies cited above are too indefinite about this. It is not easy to find levers for interventions in them. We will start by selecting two key concepts.

Key concepts

The essence of the studies cited above can be summarized as a view of organizations as networks of interdependent subunits that struggle to improve their own positions, but that need one another at the same time. The most important theoretical building blocks of the organizational model used in this book are:

1. The structure of the network. The network is composed of *parties* and their mutual *relations*.
   (a) *Parties*. What subunits can be distinguished, what is their internal structure?
   (b) *Relations*. Power and dependency relations. What links the parties? In what ways are they dependent on one another? What divides them? The nature of the relations between subunits is an extremely important element. We will discuss it at length later.
2. The culture, in the sense of *behavioural tendencies* and the '*dynamics*' of the organization.
   (a) The *behavioural tendencies*. What behavioural patterns do parties exhibit? What style of leadership is dominant? How are the mutual relations handled in decision-making and problem-solving?
   (b) The *dynamics* of the network. What tensions and problems are there between units? What stereotyped behaviours and images are dominant? What climate predominates? What problems keep recurring? This refers to unintentional outcomes, to vicious circles in which parties can become entangled.

---

* This initial sketch of the organization theory as it is used in this book shows much of the work of Elias (1971, 1984). His work was a repeated source of inspiration in the further elaboration and practical working out of the theory.

Crozier (1964) gave an example of what I mean by dynamics. He described how the 'outcome' of the strategies of groups in a bureaucratic organization was increasing rigidification and ritualization. A continuing isolation of the various levels ensued, accompanied by an increasing stereotyping on both sides, sometimes even under the guise of *esprit de corps*. *He showed that no one actually planned or intended this 'outcome'.* Gouldner (1954b) gave a good example of the almost irrepressible impulse towards a strike as the result of the strategy of the firm's new management and the counterstrategies of the subordinates.

Sometimes these dynamics lead to changes in the structure of the network. A good example is Michels' classic treatise on the 'the iron law of oligarchy'. Michels (1970) described how, in organizations which were initially democratic, such as political parties, trade unions and professional associations, small élites gradually came to dominate.

We can now represent the key concepts for an analysis of organizations schematically as shown in Figure 2.1.

These key concepts have been chosen so that they *form a framework for analysis while offering a context for interventions at the same time.* Structural interventions are likely if it is clear that the problems result from the nature of the relational network. In the following chapters we will see what forces are at work. For instance, there are organizational structures that almost invite constant and increasing bickering or a serious degree of role conflict. Restructuring the network must then be considered.

Cultural interventions attempt to influence human *behaviour* and the underlying *attitudes*. Specifying obstructive and helpful behaviour, training in certain skills and influencing the style of leadership are examples of interventions. Network dynamics in the form of chronic difficulties, gradually aggravating problems, lapsing into situations in which one begins to lose control, a rigidifying organization or increasing mutual mistrust and stereotyp-

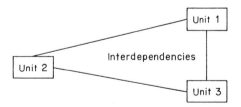

Figure 2.1   Key concepts of organization theory. (1) The structure of the network: (a) what subunits; (b) what relations link them. (2) The culture: (a) behavioural tendencies of the parties coping with relations, for instance co-operation, negotiation, 'fighting'; (b) dynamics: recurrent problems, stereotyped images, organizational climate

ing, also come under this heading. Getting a hold on these developments is a great challenge. Examples of interventions are: helping to find a manageable definition of the problem; providing a procedure to solve the problem; in role-playing or simulations, letting people feel how they are 'caught up' in the problem; clarifying the consequences of going on in the same way. Sometimes the dynamics can only be stopped by changing the organizational structure.

The boundary between behavioural tendencies and 'dynamics' is not clear cut. Both of them involve human behaviour. The more behaviour evades conscious control, the more the term 'dynamics' is applicable. For example, quite unintentionally and unplanned, people may allow themselves to be drawn further and further into an escalating conflict. Interventions aim to influence behaviour so that it becomes more 'strategic' in that it anticipates the consequences.

2.3   ELABORATION OF THE NETWORK MODEL

This compact version of the network model is only a first step. To make it applicable in practice, it is most important to differentiate relations in networks by distinguishing them into *four relational aspects*. First and foremost, we will go into *the importance of the power and dependency aspect* in relations between units. Much behaviour is of a 'political' nature, even if it is disguised otherwise. Behavioural tendencies and relevant problems are largely associated with power and dependency relations. The power and dependency aspect is central to relations; we will use the term '*one-on-three model*' to characterize the interaction between the four relational aspects.

An important part of this section is entitled 'Four tension balances in structure and culture'. It describes how the relational aspects are expressed in the structure and the culture of an organization. Their expressions result from the tension between interdependency, which drives people to co-operation, and the striving for autonomy, where the primary consideration is immediate self-interests.

The last part of this section discusses the 'dynamics' of organizations. The concept of *dynamics* in organizations can be found in the systems model, for instance, in the 'organizational goals' or in the notion that the whole is greater than the sum of the parts. In the parties model, 'dynamics' comes up in a different context, for instance, in the statement that the outcomes of intentional acts are often unintentional and unforeseen.

In this section, the dual nature of the network model will be expressed in other ways as well. In the first place, the task-oriented and socio-emotional relational aspects, which are compatible with the systems model, will be combined with the relational aspects involving power and the allocation of scarce resources. In the second place, great emphasis will be placed on the fact that there are no exclusively co-operative or competitive relations. The accents may differ, but a balance must still be found between autonomy and interdependency in each relational aspect.

Four relational aspects

Organizations are networks of co-operating and rivalling units. In some activities the emphasis is on co-operation, in other cases competition is more manifest. In other words, sometimes the common interest and the inter-dependency of organizational units are very clear, while in other cases the individual self-interests of units play a larger role.

What kinds of relations between units emphasize shared interests and co-operation and what kinds of relations show more competition and attention to self-interests? Different schools of thought in organizational sociology study types of relations that tend either to co-operation or to competition. Obviously the systems model is more attentive to relations that demand co-operation, while the parties model investigates relations that make competition more likely.

For example, Rice (1970) distinguished *task systems* and *socio-emotional systems* in the organizational system. Rice was one of the most important authors of the Tavistock group, which developed the socio-technical systems approach to organizations from the general *systems model*. This approach has gained widespread recognition for its usefulness in consulting work. Task systems consist of complexes of activities as well as the means required to perform them; socio-emotional systems are groups to which employees attach themselves and where they find moral support. On the one hand, there is the rational co-ordination and synchronization of units aimed at a broader organizational goal; on the other hand, there are the relations between units without direct consideration to their usefulness for the organization, but based on people's needs for emotional support, an identity and solidarity.

It will not be difficult to recognize this distinction in two types of relations in organizational reality. This and some other common distinctions will be discussed later (Chapter 6). What is important here is that both types of relations are associated with certain behaviour and with certain problems and frictions for which consultants are sometimes enlisted.*

1. *Instrumental relations*. People in organizations are 'means of production' for one another, in order to produce something themselves, they need the work of others. These relations are concerned with the way in which the work in organizations is divided and co-ordinated. They comprise the structure of the organization, communication patterns, methods of problem-solving and decision-making, procedures of co-ordination. They also involve the more technical side of the organization, such as through-put charts, logistics, allocating the available space, the rational use of technology. All kinds of friction can occur in these matters.

---

*We use the term 'relations' here, while we have been using the term 'relational aspects'. In an analytical sense both terms are feasible. Seeing that it is more plausible to recognize several aspects in one relation than to assume different parallel relations, we will use the term 'relational aspects' more often.

Consulting in this field builds upon the classic approach of 'scientific management'. It covers the expert method in providing high-quality solutions. More recent types of interventions aimed at improving factual communication and decision-making are also involved.

2. *Socio-emotional relations*. There are emotional ties between people in organizations, sometimes highly personal in the form of affinity or antipathy, often group-oriented in the form of positively or negatively charged common identities. Working together can create some form of team spirit and loyalty. Emotional ties in the group can become so strong that it becomes an entity with a face of its own, an 'in-group' with its affectively charged symbols in language and appearance. Here, too, all kinds of frictions can occur between the persons involved. Many interventions have been developed, primarily in the past 25 years, to make the processes at work here manifest and somewhat manageable. Increasing openness and acceptance, changing one's behaviour, learning to cope with and to express emotions, self-disclosure, feedback, confrontation meetings: it has become an approach in itself.

These two types of relations are related to the systems model. But we can point out other traditions in organizational thinking which accommodate these two types. The classic *machine model* of organizations of Taylor and his contemporaries clearly places all emphasis on instrumental relations, whereas the more recent human relations tradition of Mayo and Roethlisberger emphasizes the socio-emotional relations. The image of the organization as a *warm nest* corresponds to this tradition.

Starting from the *parties model*, we quite readily focus on relations with a more competitive bent. The two types distinguished here are power relations and negotiating relations:

3. *Power and dependency relations*. Relations among people are characterized by influencing one another's behaviour to some degree. Generally speaking, people try to increase their competence and to strengthen their position with respect to others. Dealing with the power relations of which one is a part, especially maintaining or strengthening one's own position within these relations, generally calls for a fairly cautious strategy. I call this 'political manœuvring', and sometimes 'the power game'. It is primarily a question of long-term strategies. This behaviour is more or less cautious, aimed at maintaining and acquiring status and prestige in the organization and at consolidating and further developing a strategic position. Normally this sort of behaviour remains in the background in organizations. Despite the fact that it is subtle and seldom outspoken, it is extremely important to an understanding of human behaviour in organizations.

4. *Negotiating relations*. People in organizations have to share all kinds of 'scarce resources'. We are referring to relations between units in the decision-making about resources such as jobs, space, budgets and equip-

ment. Often principles of *barter* are used ('tit for tat', 'split the difference'). Units are related to one another because, in order to take its share of the available 'cake', a unit must continue to be part of the larger whole, and because it is dependent on others in the decision-making about the division of the 'cake'.

Negotiating relations demand more overt behaviour than does the 'power game'. Some decision must be reached about the use and the allocation of scarce resources. It often involves urgent matters that must be completed within certain time limits. So one must specify one's claims, bring up arguments, have a reply or make proposals. There are some very common pitfalls in this process and, often, a tendency towards escalation. Examples: a lasting impasse or deteriorating personal relations.*

Organization theory also recognizes and elaborates these two aspects. Negotiating relations correspond to a view of the organization as a *market*, power relations to the organization as an *arena*. In my view, the concept of a *pecking order* is more appropriate than an arena. It expresses more of the underlying dynamic equilibrium and the apparent calm. The arena is too unstable and too combative.

What is the reason for this distinction into four relations? The reason is that each type of relation is associated with a different range of behavioural tendencies and problems. This implies that certain interventions are appropriate to each type of relation. We will go into the problems and possible interventions for all four types of behavioural tendencies. Power relations will be discussed in Chapter 4, negotiating relations in Chapter 5 and instrumental and socio-emotional relations will be the subject of Chapter 6.

---

* Power relations and negotiating relations differ in several aspects:

1. It was touched on above that negotiating relations are expressed more openly in the decision-making about the allocation of 'scarce resources', while power strategies generally remain more concealed. Building up a stronger power position generally takes place gradually and circumspectly, whereas claiming part of the scarce resources is very manifest. Openly laying claim to a power position will usually undermine a person's position. So there is a difference in behaviour.
2. A second difference is that a negotiating relation is more stable. There is an awareness of the mutual dependency; one recognizes the position of the opponent, although there is a tendency to test it now and then. *Shifts in position take place away from and not at the negotiating table.*
3. In negotiating relations, the awareness of this mutual dependency goes together with a *certain symmetry in the balance of power*. The more asymmetrical the balance of power is, the less will we have to do with negotiating. Other behaviour, such as instructing or 'requesting' vs passiveness or 'retreating', then becomes more likely (Rubin and Brown, 1975, pp. 214–34).

Points 2 and 3 tell us that the power relation, which crystallizes at a certain point, forms a frame of reference in which negotiating takes place. So power relations certainly play a role as a very important aspect, and naturally people will now and then try to alter them a little, but in negotiating something else is primary: making a decision about an allocation problem.

The 'one-on-three' model

Which of the four relational aspects is the most important is debatable. There are both authors and consultants who equate organizational effectiveness and flexibility with the quality of the socio-emotional aspect. Extensive training programmes to stimulate openness, to break through inhibitions and to develop the skill of honest feedback are undertaken to achieve this. By now this approach has had its heyday. The idea that relations between units sometimes have a negotiating aspect has recently begun to gain acceptance. Developing negotiating skills has become a normal subject in management training courses. The 'classic' view that primary attention should go to breakdowns in the instrumental and technical aspects—to the effective use of technology in clarifying the organizational structure and to procedures of coordination—is still strong.

We take the power and dependency aspect of relations to be the most important. The tension between autonomy and mutual dependency is central to this aspect; this tension is expressed in the other aspects as well. Furthermore, power relations are the most clearly connected with problems which are more or less chronic in organizations. A great deal of behaviour in organizations can very well be explained from power relations. Power relations can also impede organizational change and adaptation more than can socio-emotional frictions or a lack of instrumental expertise. These assertions may sound somewhat cryptic; they will be elaborated below and in Chapters 3 and 4.

We can express the interaction between the four relational aspects by the term 'one-on-three model'. *The power and dependency aspect can be seen as a bedding in which the other three aspects are anchored, although the bedding is sometimes influenced by the other three.** Figure 2.2 is an attempt to express this idea.

---

*The following four points once again briefly summarize the reasons for the separate and central position of power relations:

1. Power strategies are more covert than the strategies that people use in the other three kinds of relations. Behaviour aimed at strengthening one's position is evidently still 'taboo'. And yet much behaviour in organizations can very well be explained by 'political' motives.

2. The problems associated with power relations are more fundamental and more difficult to solve than the problems in the other three relational types (see Chapter 3).

3. The other three relations are more strongly influenced by the power relations than vice versa. Negotiating relations are embedded in power relations in a certain way (see note on p. 15 and Chapter 5). In much of this literature, especially on organizational development, instrumental and above all socio-emotional relations assume a symmetry in power relations, or at least a high degree of interdependency. Sometimes it even seems that the other three relations are only possible in certain power and dependency relations.

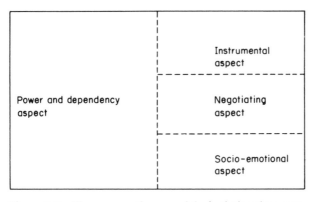

Figure 2.2   The one-on-three model of relational aspects

To explain the interaction between the four relational aspects, it is necessary to define power more specifically. It is primarily important to understand
how power and dependency form a kind of symbiosis.

Power and dependency

Mulder (1977, p. 15) defined the exercise of power as 'determining or direct-
ing the behaviour of others to some degree'. The essence of this definition lies
in the fact that one person influences the behaviour of another. Power is a
relational fact. We can see it as a certain type of relation, but also as an aspect
of all relations between people. Power is never absolutely one-sided. But
power in a relation may be very unequally divided.

We can conceptualize a power relation as a balance: a tension balance
between units (Elias, 1970). This balance may be tipped to one side, so that
one person has authority over another. Or it may be more or less in horizontal
equilibrium. The term 'balance' points up what is important here: power
relations have some instability and are liable to fluctuate. But they are also
rather stable, even if power is unequally divided. The balance is a dynamic
equilibrium; this fits in with the network model and with organizational reality.

Parties try to maintain and strengthen their positions. Fluctuations are
normal. Some preoccupation with power relations and with strategic ploys
imparts an inherent dynamism to relations in organizations.

Power relations are connected to dependency relations. Emerson (1962)

4. The most important reason is that the structure of power and dependency in
   organizations is clearly related to: behavioural tendencies such as style of leadership, employee dedication; and to dynamics as recurrent problems and organizational climate.

saw power as the reverse of dependency, and this is the view we will adopt. This caused Hickson *et al.* (1971, p. 217) to pose the following question: 'If dependency in a social relation is the reverse of power, then the crucial unanswered question in organizations is: what factors function to vary dependency and so to vary power?' Hickson *et al.* answered this question as follows. By definition, the division of work in organizations means dependency among units, but some units are less dependent than others. Three factors determine the degree to which organizational units are dependent:

1. Uncertainty;
2. Substitutability;
3. Centrality.

Uncertainty refers to a lack of information about the future. Being able to respond to the uncertainties of others in the fields of input, control of throughput and sales renders a subunit more powerful than other subunits. Substitutability is the degree to which alternatives are available for the activities of a particular organizational unit. The harder it is to find a substitute, the greater is the unit's power. Centrality is the degree of interdependence, of being interwoven with other units; it is also the interest the unit has in the survival of the organization. The more central the position, the greater the power.

The advantage of this approach to power is that the nature of the network between parties is the focus of attention. Centrality and substitutability are especially workable concepts in this sense. They point to network characteristics that can have direct consequences for the power relations.

To borrow Emerson's (1962) definition, the degree of dependency is determined by two factors:

1. The importance the unit attaches to the activities of another unit;
2. The substitutability of those activities and the degree to which alternatives are available.

This reasoning is intended to illuminate how *power is interwoven with other relational aspects*. Emerson's symbiosis of power and dependency helps to make this clear. Instrumental, socio-emotional and negotiating aspects influence the power balance and vice versa. Hickson *et al.* (1971) showed that task dependence in networks may be understood as centrality, substitutability and the control of uncertainty, and thus as a power relation. Great dependency on the expertise of subordinates in a hierarchical situation will tilt the power balance in a more horizontal direction. In the reverse situation, instrumental regrouping of tasks by management often has consequences for the power chances of those involved.

How socio-emotional ties influence power relations is shown by Blau (1962), White (1961) and Lincoln and Miller (1979). Lincoln and Miller investigated what clusters of 'primary ties' and certain aspects of power occurred in several different organizations. Power relations can be socio-emotionally charged: this will be discussed in Chapter 4.

Negotiating behaviour is very clearly influenced by power relations. Negotiating can only take place when there is a certain power equilibrium. Parties are mutually dependent in the sense that they must do business with each other; alternatives are not available or can only be found with great difficulty. How the power balance is of influence during negotiating will be elaborated in Chapter 5.

Conclusion

A person exercises power when he influences the behaviour of another person. Power is a relational characteristic. Dependency is the reverse of power. One person is dependent on another if:

(a) he regards the activities of the other as important;
(b) it is very difficult to find a substitute for those activities.

The greater the dependency, the more the behaviour of the one is determined by the other. Other relational aspects may very well be considered in isolation, but they also affect the power balance. This emphasizes once again the 'mixed' nature of relations: the aspects can be distinguished but not separated.

This consideration of power and dependency relations may perhaps make the reader think that it will be very difficult to make any more systematic statements about how power relations work, because of the complexity of intertwined dependencies in organizations. But we must not exaggerate this. Many people in organizations know quite exactly and fairly unambiguously how the power relations lie for them. People in organizations often work hard at keeping their 'power charts' up to date. Shifts in position, changes and promotions, assignment of important projects—these are all things which are immediately registered, talked about and considered with a view to their consequences for the power network and one's own position. These are the power relations we refer to, for they are our guide-lines for our daily activities. Maintaining and strengthening one's position in terms of the subjectively perceived and registered power relations forms the rationale behind a wide variety of behaviours.

Much of the behaviour in organizations can be linked to a number of important problems in organizations in this way. The power game has its own rules, here briefly expressed by the term 'political manœuvring'. This term indicates that it is usually played indirectly and with circumspection, which is a power strategy in itself, because too openly trying to strengthen one's position will only serve to undermine it.

It is very important to be aware that the energy invested in 'power games' can very well be applied for the benefit of the organization. Some organizational conditions make it possible to apply the energy of the power game to achieving greater effectiveness in the organization, and other organizational conditions allow the struggle for power to become mired in endless tugs-of-war and fruitless bickering.

Four tension balances in structure and culture

Each type of relation is seen here as a relation which exhibits *both* co-operative *and* competitive impulses *simultaneously*. These impulses are anchored in the *structure* and in the *culture* of the organization. There is always a tension between wanting some degree of autonomy vs the reality of being interdependent. This directs our attention to the central relational aspect: power and dependency between units. It governs the other three aspects. We shall see how this tension is expressed in each of the four aspects.

Power and dependency aspect

Units in an organization have interests of their own. Units aim to consolidate and strengthen their strategic positions with respect to other units. They generally strive for more authority and responsibility. At the very least, they try to safeguard their position. At the same time units are mutually dependent. They are part of a larger whole. Without that whole they would be functioning in a vacuum. Often, too, they need the strength of the totality. Without the totality they simply would not survive. The tension in this relational aspect between the impulses towards co-operation and competition can be expressed schematically as shown in Figure 2.3.

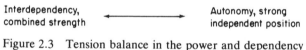

Interdependency,   Autonomy, strong
combined strength   independent position

Figure 2.3   Tension balance in the power and dependency
aspect

Instrumental aspect

Subunits of an organization are also linked to one another in an instrumental way. They need one another's outputs in order to generate an output themselves. Effectively linking outputs and developing mutually accepted decisions about product improvement are often a source of friction. Units must arrive at agreements about the division and co-ordination of tasks. The throughput of products must be organized. Unambiguous norms for quality must be agreed upon, met and tested. Adaptations and product improvements must be introduced smoothly and effectively. In short, quite a lot must take place before the organization can function like *a well-oiled machine*. The problem in the decision-making is to develop sufficient support and acceptance. The preferences of the separate units must come together in a workable consensus. There is the tension balance between the need for consensus, so that things run smoothly, and the need for specialisms and expertise in certain fields, with preferences of their own. In this relational aspect the co-operative and competitive impulses are expressed in Figure 2.4.

Consensus   ◄————————————►   Preferences of one's own

Figure 2.4   Tension balance in the instrumental aspect

Socio-emotional aspect

Units in an organization develop their own identities. These identities are sometimes on a tense footing with the identity of the larger whole. In spite of this, some organizations succeed in developing a very strong 'we-feeling', while leaving sufficient leeway for the expression of 'peculiarities' of units. Sometimes, however, the group climate and group obligations can be so suffocating that a unit feels its own identity is being trampled on. This aspect is also characterized by a paradoxical contrast: on the one hand there is the need for an overall identity, on the other hand there is the strong emotional support which can come from being part of a closely knit group. In fairly small organizations these two impulses can be united. For hierarchically structured and broadly differentiated large organizations, this is a difficult job. And yet some organizations succeed in uniting their subunits by means of strongly developed affective ties. The two paradoxical impulses in this relational aspect are summarized in Figure 2.5.

We-feeling   ◄————————————►   Own identity

Figure 2.5   Tension balance in the socio-emotional aspect

Negotiating aspect

Negotiating relations are characterized by the tension between attempting to increase one's own share in the available resources and, on the other hand, the interest one has in making the total resources as large as possible. Organizational units have many different wants as to available resources such as budgets, personnel, space, furnishings, computer time and other facilities. They also have their wishes about interesting work, certain projects and responsibilities. If all these wishes are taken together, they generally far exceed what is possible and available. Still, there are strong impulses for each unit to increase its own share in the available resources. At the same time it is in everyone's interests that the available resources are utilized where they can be expected to provide the most benefit. For the larger the total benefit, the more there is to divide. There is an apparent contrast between the powers at work in this aspect. The tension balance between these two impulses is expressed in Figure 2.6.

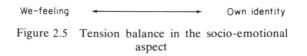

Maximizing   ◄————————————►   Maximizing
total benefits   one's own share

Figure 2.6   Tension balance in the negotiating aspect

So far in our discussion of the four relational aspects we have not explicitly used the distinction we made earlier between structure and culture. The relational aspects have a structural and a cultural side: they take a *tangible form* in the structure of the organization. In the culture they are expressed in *the manner in which* they are dealt with; these are the behavioural tendencies and the resulting dynamics. In Table 2.2 we give a few examples of the structural and cultural sides of the four relational aspects.

Table 2.2   Structure and culture in relation to the four relational aspects

	Power and dependency	Instrumental	Socio-emotional	Negotiating
Structure	The division of powers and responsibilities	The organization of the work, procedures of co-ordination	The crystallized network of informal relations, symbols of identity	The norms as they are set down for matters of allocation such as incomes and investments
Culture	The manner in which the division of powers and responsibilities is dealt with	The manner in which work relations are dealt with and problems solved	The manner in which acceptance and trust, a 'we-feeling', are cultivated	The manner in which one behaves and makes decisions in allocating scarce resources

Behaviour in organizations

Behaviour in organizations is characterized by the tension between co-operation and competition. It seeks an optimum between mutual dependency and autonomy. Behaviour can be conceptualized by the manner in which people deal with the tension balance in their interrelations. This means a balancing act between co-operative and competitive impulses. We can think of these balances as polarities in the sense of the definition given by the *Concise Oxford Dictionary: possession of two poles having contrary qualities*.

This concept also expresses something of the paradoxical, the seeming opposition of the poles. Both poles are important. Behaviour seeks an optimum. This search is an interplay. A dynamic equilibrium comes about: a balance of tension. If the balance tips to one side, behaviour becomes aggressive; if it shifts to the other side, behaviour becomes too indulgent, and one's own specific contribution does not really show or matter.

The structure of an organization can allow the equilibrium to tilt to one of the two poles. In the following chapter we will see that neither the employees nor the organization benefit by this: *both* co-operative *and* competitive impulses are important. This 'both–and' nature of relations imparts energy and vitality. A balance of tension between both impulses is only possible if *both* the mutual dependency *and* the autonomy are dealt with in the relations between organizational units.

Forming concepts

In my view, the 'mixed' nature of relations is not so difficult to understand in itself, but we have not yet found the proper terms to express it. The evidence that human relations are mixed is overwhelming, but our thoughts keep reverting to 'either competition or co-operation'. *We lack images and concepts to map out and to grasp the area between co-operation and competition.* We have too few metaphors with which we can conceptualize these phenomena. We have used terms such as 'mixed', 'dynamic equilibrium', 'balance', 'dilemma', 'paradox', 'tension balance' and 'polarity'. All of these concepts express the characteristic alliance of co-operation and competition.

Familiar terms are still scarce. It is my impression that, once we become accustomed to concepts for this 'mixed area', it will be easier to avoid the pitfalls that lie here.

Dynamics

One of the key concepts in this network model of organizations is the 'dynamics'. The dynamics express themselves in 'unplanned problems' between units. It is a good idea to define this key concept more closely, because it gives us another opportunity to bring the systems model and the parties model closer together.

A strong side of the systems model is its attention to phenomena that cannot be explained from the intentions of the actions of the parties involved. In a certain sense, organizations have lives of their own, objectives of their own. They have their own dynamics, independent of the interests of the composing parts. This understandably leads to the use of more impersonal concepts. The systems model points out that a great many organizational processes are relatively autonomous of the motives and actions of the parties involved.

Many organizational processes may be relatively autonomous of the parties involved, but they still result from human actions. But the relations are so complex, the dependency chains so intricate, that it becomes more and more difficult for the individual parties to understand the whole, let alone to control it. Even if a person acts with certain intentions and even if he aims at certain effects, the outcome of his planned and intentional action is but all too often unintentional and unplanned. In his portrayal of a series of game models of increasing complexity, Elias (1971) showed how we tend to form concepts which say much about how we perceive such a situation—we do not experience events as the result of planned and intentional human action—but little about what is actually happening. Perhaps a few quotations can show how our conceptual faculties start shuttling back and forth between the parties and the systems model. Elias (1971, p. 99) pointed out that the 'players' in increasingly complex networks gradually alter their ideas about the course of the game:

> Rather than reducing the course of the game to individual moves, their assimilation of events gradually starts to develop into more impersonal concepts that take more account of the relative autonomy of the players than of the motives of individual players. But working out such vehicles to accommodate the increasing awareness that the course of the game is uncontrollable for the players themselves is a long and arduous process. The comparisons people use constantly shift back and forth between the idea that the course of the game can be reduced to the actions of idividual players, and the idea that there is something superhuman about it. *For a long time it has been extremely difficult for the players to understand that the uncontrollability of the course of the game for them, which they readily perceive as something 'superhuman', results from their mutual dependency, from being interdependent as players and from the tensions and conflicts that go along with this* [italics mine].
>
> The action theories [these are variants of the parties model] do not come to grips with the questions brought up here of the nature of human interdependencies and of power balances and their implications. At most, they simply assume that intentional interactions have unintended consequences. But they obscure the fact central to the theory and practice of sociology that every intentional interaction is based on unintended human interdependencies (Elias, 1971, p. 103).

And a little further:

> a game which is the exclusive result of the interaction of the individual moves of many players takes a course that none of the individual players intended, determined or foresaw, so that precisely the reverse is true: it is the unintentional course of the game that determines the moves of the individual players (Elias, 1971, p. 103).

So we may see both parties and systems models as a typical phase in the development of our thinking which parallels the rise of more and more complex networks.

The dynamics of 'unintended human interdependencies' will be explained in Chapters 3 and 4. By keeping this idea foremost in our minds, we can fit an important 'systems' phenomenon into the present network model.

2.4   THE 'PARTIES IN A SYSTEM' MODEL

We began this chapter with Lammers's schematic summary of the systems and parties models. We also emphasized the insight that *social relations are of a mixed nature*. We have endeavoured to elaborate this insight in the previous sections in working towards an *integration of the parties and the systems models*. We saw a second important impulse to integration in Elias's insights about the *'dynamics'* of human networks. There is a relationship between network structure and behavioural tendencies in organizations.

By *combining these two insights* we have attempted to effect an integration. This has not been merely a theoretical exercise, for we also want an organizational model that provides something to go on in answering the question how we can order organizations as effectively as possible. More specifically it is about the question: 'What types of "blends" in the relations between units set positive dynamics in motion?' An example of what we are trying to work out here is concisely expressed in the following quotation from Gouldner (1954a):

'The more an organisation offers leeway to parties to pursue their own interests, the greater is the tendency to self-preservation and the more durable is the organisation as a whole.'

In this quotation we see an interesting mix of autonomy and mutual dependency. The tension balance between these two impulses is the primary characteristic of relations between units in our network theory. This corresponds to what Lammers calls the dual nature of organizations: 'It is a cooperative relation and a market plus arena at the same time!'

Lastly, I want to place these attempts at integration in a 'parties in a system' model into Lammers's table with which we began this chapter (Table 2.1). I have tried to fill in the first three pairs of propositions so as to clarify the role of tension balances of contrasting impulses. (Figure 2.7).

The integration is achieved by adapting Lammers's three viewpoints to characteristics of both the systems and the parties models. The model thus embraces the dual nature of organizations. The proper 'blend' is expressed by the maxim which 'bridges the gap' in the tension balance. These maxims are based on the duality, but at the same time they express something more: they not only *combine* polar characteristics, but also *strengthen* the tension between the two poles. This can be an outstanding characteristic of organizations. *The object is a certain articulation of both the incentives towards one another and the incentives away from one another!* These incentives can be influenced by *structuring* the relations between units in a certain way; they can also be influenced via the organizational *culture* by, for example, changing behaviour patterns such as the style of management. It is the development of both types of impulses that makes organizations function more effectively and sets in motion 'positive dynamics': a development of the dualistic nature of organizations! We will discuss this in the next chapter. We will describe the structural and cultural elements relevant to the four relational aspects in such detail that they can provide a firm basis for making choices in change strategies towards more effective organizations.

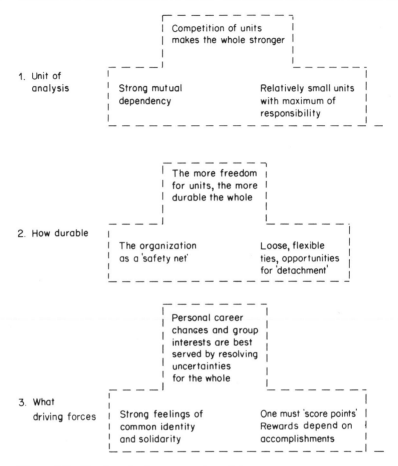

Figure 2.7   The 'parties in a system' model

2.5   SUMMARY

We see organizations as *networks* of groups and individuals. The game for power and the decision-making about the allocation of scarce resources, traditional points of emphasis in the parties model of organisations, fit well into a network model. It is not surprising that these two aspects have a fairly competitive ring. Negotiating, 'political' manœuvring, forming coalitions, lobbying—they are all activities appropriate to power and negotiating relations.

If we concentrate on the task-oriented and socio-emotional relations, then our eye falls on entirely different activities: rational decision-making, the structuring and co-ordination of tasks, improving co-operation, team-building. In the organization theory described here both sorts of relations are important. Organizations are mixed. For the organization theory described here it is even more important that this mix also exists within relations. There is always a balance between co-operative *and* competitive forces. The specific organizational structure and culture may give autonomy and rivalry more opportunities; in other cases the mutual dependencies are predominant.

The rationale of the distinction into four relational aspects is that it fits very well to several proven categories in organizational theory and to different behavioural tendencies, problems and interventions. Examples of common problems in the relations between units are: co-ordination of tasks is far from perfect; personal irritations put work relations under pressure; the allocation of available resources becomes deadlocked; power struggles between departments result in an ongoing struggle for competence and authority. Essentially, the four relational aspects with their corresponding behavioural tendencies may exhibit a wide variety of disturbances, and sometimes serious and acute problems. A consultant will do well to distinguish the four problem areas when intervening.

The power and dependency aspect of relations is seen as central. This is expressed in the term 'the one-on-three model'. It is so important because it affects the other three relational aspects. It is also most clearly associated with recurring problems and with the dynamics of organizations.

3 Change Strategy

3.1 INTRODUCTION

A change strategy must contain two elements. (1) It must give a general outline of the *goals of change*: ideas about the structure and culture to be achieved. Section 3.2 describes this. (2) It must provide an *approach*: the way in which changes can be achieved. Section 3.3 discusses this.

The *goals* of change are related to the organization theory. The *approach* mainly involves the structuring and integration of concrete interventions. Using the diagram from Chapter 1, we can picture these links as shown in Figure 3.1.

3.2 CHANGE STRATEGY: GOALS

This section explains the *goals* of the change strategy. The goals pertain to the desired organizational structure and culture. They fit into the perspective of the organization theory used here.

Making organizations more manageable and 'vital'

Is there such a thing as an organizational culture that deserves emulation? Are there statements to be made about the direction in which an organizational culture ought to develop? In other words, can we indicate what conditions influence behavioural tendencies and dynamics positively?

Every organization is a complex and constantly evolving entity of disciplines, departments, hierarchical levels and functional groups. All these units are linked by a network of interdependencies and transactions. Even if the organization or the unit in the organization is small and not very complex, it is still a part of a network of dependencies.

It is difficult to bring into focus the dynamics of such complicated and extensive networks. The most immediate explanation for these dynamics lies

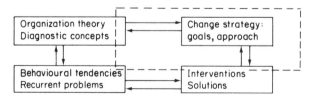

Figure 3.1   The contents of Chapter 3

in the positions and the behaviour of those directly involved. The game models of Elias (1971) show how, even in relatively simple structures, people can become 'trapped' in the dynamics which they themselves have set in motion. Getting a grasp on the dynamics of networks, to which a consultant may also belong, is a great challenge. The basic question is how to achieve the regulation and co-ordination of these networks, how to bring about *dynamics* in the desired direction. The desired direction implies the effective and deliberate use of resources in satisfying the demands of the environment—in business and industry, in a way suited to coping with the competition. Organizations that do this are organizations that function with a certain *vitality*.

Vitality is a broad concept. It incorporates effective and competitive functioning. It also expresses the innovative ability of an organization. At the same time it relates to the motivation and the creativity with which people at many different levels do their work. *It is my conviction that people can learn to manage the problems they encounter in working together; first and foremost, the problem of mobilizing the energy needed for survival and renewal, which is potentially present in every group of people working together.*

In illustration, we will first give two *examples* of 'vital' organizations. Then we will describe some *characteristics* these examples have *in common*. These characteristics will be worked out in detail in the important section entitled 'Strengthening productive tension', which is based on the four tension balances between the units of an organization as described in the preceding chapter.

Examples

Some organizations 'stimulate' endless frictions and fruitless internal bickering; the effect is stagnation. Other organizations have a mobilizing effect; they arouse energy in their employees. Three examples of the second type follow:

1. A *pumping machinery* supplier had to make a difficult decision. The company was growing. The choice was between expanding the present company or establishing another similar company. It seemed simple. The former solution would require considerably lower investment. The economies of scale would make it possible to produce at lower costs. And yet this manager hesitated. He knew that these calculations did not include several factors which were more difficult to gauge. He thought of the losses that would be incurred by a much larger version of the present company because of less sight of the whole, longer lines of communication, continuing bureaucratization, greater anonymity of employees, alienation at the top, more interference from staff services, discontent and start-up problems that would result from such sweeping changes in the well-oiled company, loss of flexibility and motivation. He also saw the present informal pattern of interpersonal relations becoming clouded. He decided to make the second choice, although it looked more expensive on the face of it. The

advantages he saw were: (1) avoiding the negative factors mentioned; and (2) a productive tension between the two plants from which both of them could profit. The second point, especially, has proved to be more and more advantageous. Managers of the two companies regularly exchange experiences and ideas from which both companies derive much benefit.

2. A subsidiary of a multinational company produced semi-manufactures for other sectors of the company. The subsidiary received a wide range of facilities and many forms of support from the company. The company as a whole had a specific identity and culture of its own which extended to this subsidiary as well; the employees were quite proud of it. The subsidiary was bound by central guide-lines in terms of employment; its management was obliged to follow company policy in management development. But the internal organization structure and the production process were left to the subsidiary's own discretion. Investments to improve the production process were evaluated at company level only along general lines; the subsidiary's budget was generous. This was offset by the fact that its sales to other company sectors were in no way guaranteed. The subsidiary had to compete with other manufacturers in the company *and* outside of it! In a period of economic decline, the subsidiary demonstrated its flexibility by making several well-timed adaptations in its product range.

3. A publishing company had recently been through an internal reorganization into market-oriented profit centres: groups of publishers who together cover a certain market, such as sports and recreation, culture, economy and finance. The groups were made responsible for all types of publications in their field. In the past, the organization had been much less clearcut; emphasis had been on product-oriented units, each with a particular type of publication. Some had concentrated on periodicals, others on books, others again on loose-leaf editions. The new units were given monthly information on indicators important to them such as costs, including salaries, and turnovers. To strengthen the market position of the company, management faced the difficult problem of strengthening the entrepreneurship of the units: 'How can we encourage the entrepreneur in the company?' To bring this into practice, a few important conditions were set down in the form of questions:

- To what extent do units learn from one another's successes and failures?
- Do the units exhibit enough comradely exchange and support to strengthen tendencies to success?
- Does the monthly information give a realistic picture of success and failure tendencies; how might it be adjusted; how used to ensure that the maximum benefit is drawn from it?
- To what extent are there rewards for outstanding results?
- Are there enough opportunities for initiatives and experiments?

In several workshops the conditions were converted into general practical guide-lines with those directly involved. Management then stimulated bringing them into practice and further elaborating them. These impulses turned out to set in motion an increasingly successful internal entrepreneurship. The organization began to acquire a new vitality.

Common characteristics

From the point of view of the organization theory used here, we will now pick out the essence of these examples. They show that the relations between and within the units of the organization were conditioned in a certain manner. These conditions set in motion a dynamic process, a process which contributed to the success of the organization. This process can be summarized as follows.

- *Within* units a greater sense of interdependency developed. The more manifest need to compete and to survive stimulated internal solidarity, motivation and an entrepreneurial climate.
- *Between* units a productive tension developed through the exchange and comparison of results. Interdependency was reinforced by devices such as horizontal job rotation, developing common goals and fostering informal personal contacts.

These examples show that a high energy level in organizations is achieved by strengthening both the interdependency and the autonomy of organizational units. The managers involved focused on a certain productive tension between organizational units, thus strengthening the dual nature of the organization. The arsenal of concrete management and organizational principles which can be applied to achieve this will be described in the following section.

Strengthening productive tension

How can the dual nature of organizations be strengthened? To clarify this, we will describe two types of interventions and characteristics:

1. Interventions and characteristics that strengthen the *autonomy* of units: greater independence, more pronounced self-interests, more ways of identifying with one's own unit, more chances to be led by one's own preferences.
2. Interventions and characteristics that strengthen the *interdependency* of units: emphasis on the interest of the whole, intensive mutual exchange to learn from one other, strengthening the 'we-feeling', emphasis on consensus.

What we are dealing with here is influencing the tension balance in *the power and dependency relations* between units (Figure 3.2). We shall first point out the most important structural interventions, and then go on to explain the cultural interventions.

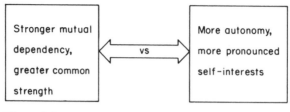

Figure 3.2

Structure

What *structure* combines self-interests with organizational interests? What interventions and characteristics can bring both impulses into one line? Below is a brief outline of the organizational structure we have in mind.

An important recommendation is to create relatively autonomous managers who are able to respond directly to the market. An organization has to be structured in units that run distinct product categories, preferably units with their own profit responsibility. Often a large degree of autonomy can be achieved in many fields: internal structure, internal resources, client and market-oriented operation, product development. Staff facilities, too, can often be decentralized and function under the management of the units.

Several devices may be employed to balance this stimulation of autonomy with closer interdependency:

- Systematic horizontal job rotation for managers. In this way, organizations develop generalists and all-round managers with an increased awareness of what units stand for. Hobbyism and escalating rivalries have fewer opportunities if a person stands a chance of becoming part of an adjacent organizational unit. An additional advantage is that people will considerably expand their networks of personal relations throughout the organization over the years. Horizontal job rotation can be particularly important at an executive level. It effectively curtails the tendency to established strongholds of managers whose special expertise has made them invincible in their field.

Other ways of strengthening the organization as a whole are:

- A company policy to prevent forced dismissals. If something goes wrong in a unit, openings elsewhere in the organization are sought and found for the personnel. In addition, centralized personnel facilities for recreation, housing, pension provisions, health care, study and training, etc.
- Central facilities that subunits would never be able to afford in fields such as research and development, automated systems and venture capital.
- A management that controls along general lines, one that sets out a strategic course and sometimes mediates and bridges differences of opinion between units. If necessary, it makes decisions to avoid unproductive

bickering. This central management also encourages *balanced relations* between units.

- A very important characteristic is that hierarchical interference and control remain limited and are structured in a certain way. In general, we may state that control focuses predominantly on the output; there is relatively little interference with the input and throughput. This is made possible by means of norms and index figures which establish ratios between costs/ personnel resources (input) and yields (output). As long as a unit manages to achieve them, it need expect no further interference. It may be even simpler to set transfer prices to be used for charging the costs of internal supplies. If, in addition to the basis of comparison of the price/achievement ratios, units may make use of the services of different suppliers inside their company, or even outside of it, this forms a powerful built-in test of internal efficiency and effectiveness. Norms and index figures are really no longer necessary!

- A systematic exchange and comparison of results of units. The following example of the meetings of a Japanese director with his division managers shows how a competitive spirit can benefit the organization as a whole:

  Division managers also attend quarterly peer reviews at which their summary operating results are shared in front of one another. Divisions are grouped into A, B, C or D classes, the A (outstanding) divisions make their presentations first, the Ds last. In the words of one of the attendants, 'There is little need to expose people in public. Where your division stands in the ranking and whether you are moving up or down is a powerful motivator. No one individual or division is cruelly singled out or openly embarrassed in these meetings, but every division implicated in a poor quarterly performance leaves determined not to face that embarrassment again' (Pascale and Athos, 1981, p. 62).

This intervention is so ingenious because it incorporates *both greater autonomy and increased interdependency*. Less direct intervention from above is needed: units become more and more independent. The same Japanese manager expressed this as follows:

  When I meet with my managers it is seldom formal. We communicate knee to knee. A crucial element is their independence, so, however pointed my questions and direct the implications, I refrain from giving orders. We must respect the pride of different individuals and honor the traditions of their companies (Pascale and Athos, 1981, p. 71).

At the same time there is more horizontal exchange: by stimulating one another and learning from one another, units profit more from one another's experiences and ideas.

The two-fold nature of this intervention is striking in another respect: making results manifest while exchanging and comparing them undoubtedly strengthens *rivalry* and *competition* between units. In the above example from

Japan this competition for results is even honed to a fine point. But it is compensated by opportunities to stimulate and learn from one another. *This demands co-operation! The managers who excel at it—who do not hide themselves, who are open about the factors behind their successes and who show a certain eagerness in learning from others—have the best chances for promotion.* This has something of a paradox: self-interests are benefited by serving the whole!

Culture

We see here that in addition to structural interventions, a certain *culture* is consciously developed and encouraged: a culture of *both* individual prominence *and* strong common ties. An example: an American company 'Jewel', with stores all over the USA, speaks very emphatically of its 'interdependent company': it is a right but also an obligation to make use of one another's knowledge. Albert Heijn, head of a Dutch supermarket chain, remarked in this connection: 'The divisions, the operating companies are fully self-supporting. The director of Miro cannot be compelled to consult Ahold. But if he consistently refuses to do so, I think it will be noted on his conduct sheet. . . . Our policy is that operating companies may certainly show some overlap, may operate their own markets, stimulate *and* compete with one another' (Cozijnsen and Ezerman, 1984, p. 15).

Examples of such a **'both–and' culture** come from the American companies General Motors (GM) and 3M. A special place is reserved where each evening everyone deposits a file showing the research he is working on. Others can thumb through it, make comments and give advice. This is also a strong mixture: people are encouraged to distinguish themselves by always working on something inspiring, because everyone can see. At the same time there is a climate of joint support, exchange and stimulation.

Such a culture can be stimulated in other ways as well. A main factor is to encourage willingness to experiment and internal entrepreneurship. This gives employees and units ample opportunity to work out promising ideas. Such a culture is also encouraged by a strong focus on developing and profiling the talents of employees: an active training policy. Broadly put, people have the freedom to act according to their own judgement. Non-conformity is even encouraged. A good illustration is the 'skunks' and 'skunkworks' advocated by Peters and Austin (1985). Skunks are innovative but obstinate employees; they are necessary for renewal. Sensible managers leave such nuisances free to set up 'skunkworks': groups of people who work on highly promising projects. Peters and Austin gave an almost endless series of practical examples to demonstrate how such pertinacious employees are of vital importance to a great many different companies. They also showed that it is not enough to encourage people to distinguish themselves, to try something new. The other side of the coin is that the organization must form a strong safety net to catch those who fall. People take risks more readily when they know they will be well supported in the final analysis. This is an excellent example of strengthening both the tendencies towards autonomy and towards interdependency! It brings about an innovative climate in the organization, and the organization as a whole is better capable of flexibly meeting challenges in the environment.

Two examples follow of reorganizations which exemplify the above characteristics and interventions:

In a retail company there was a long-standing rivalry between purchasing and sales. Its effects were stereotyping on both sides, fruitless bickering and suboptimization. The sales and purchasing departments were recently integrated and grouped into profit centres. These new departments became responsible for their own results. After a difficult start-up phase, mutual relations clearly improved. More and more people started identifying with their profit centres. They also started trying to distinguish themselves from other profit centres in their results.

In a construction company, a process of decentralization was set in motion a few years ago. Diminishing results had made a more flexible client-oriented organization necessary for the mere survival of the firm. The central staff was gradually thinned out and many ex-members were moved to regional branches, which became more and more independent. Only what was strictly necessary remained central, a matter in which the management of the regional offices also had an important say. Every now and then the remaining central services put up a hard fight when they feel that important specialized activities are being threatened. The reaction of the top management is just as simple as it is efficacious: keep working on it but operate from the regional offices!

Two more aspects of these examples should be mentioned:

1. The important role of administrative automation in both reorganizations. Direct and comprehensible feedback of indices and results turned out to be highly motivating. The opportunity to compare results continually induced people to work towards improvement and adaptation. The stronger the bond between units, so that people could learn from one another and help one another on points where they were obviously doing better, the stronger was this effect. Here we once again see a remarkable blend of competition and co-operation.
2. Seen in retrospect, the organizational changes described may perhaps seem simple and logical. It is easy to misjudge this. Both cases involved change processes that took years. The—often intuitive—search for balanced relations characterized by the proper productive tension has still not been completed. Along the way, many of those directly involved have had well-founded doubts about whether or not they were on the right track.

The central tension balance of 'dependency–autonomy' affects the other three relational aspects in different ways. We will now discuss how the tension balance can be influenced in these three aspects.

Instrumental aspect

This aspect involves the tension balance between the necessity for consensus, so that things run smoothly, and the need for specializations and expertise, with preferences of their own. Organizations have traditionally solved this dilemma by leaving decisions to managers. Employees and specialists may make suggestions, managers take decisions. One of the most important developments of recent years is that alternatives have been found on an increasingly large scale for this simple straightforward system. This is not so surprising in view of the very high costs of constant hierarchical monitoring. Recurrent problems in this context are resistance to change and lack of motivation among employees. Enthusiasm, willingness to adapt, concern about the product and entrepreneurship can become very scarce at lower levels in an organization. Chapter 4 will describe the dynamics inherent in hierarchical structures. These 'spontaneous' dynamics can be deflected by *structural interventions* as described in the previous section:

1. Replacing pyramidal, functionally structured organizations by more decentralized, federalist organizational forms; this yields distinct units with clear-cut responsibilities of their own, including profit.
2. At the same time, restricting hierarchical interference and control, in particular by introducing horizontal exchange and comparison.
3. Other structural ways of countering the detrimental effects of great hierarchical authority are giving lower echelons a say in appointments and developing frameworks for employee participation in the decision-making, such as the works council. The following gives an interesting example of how consensus formation can be structurally influenced.

General Motors is building a new automobile factory in Tennessee. Starting in 1987, 400 000 motor cars will be manufactured there every year. The factory will ultimately cost $5 billion. The organizational structure this factory will have is already known down to the minutest details (*Business Week*, 1985).

The first group, and lowest in rank, will be called a work unit: teams of six to fifteen workers, all of whom are union members, and who elect a sort of 'councillor' from their midst. The team members decide who will perform what job. The team is responsible for the tools and the parts required, and members will regulate their holidays and days off among themselves. Each team is to have a personal computer for keeping stocks and production results.

But their responsibility will go much further. The teams will do quality checks, keep an eye on the variable costs and make suggestions to produce certain things more cheaply or efficiently. These suggestions are passed on to the financial department, which is obliged to reach consensus with the team in question. Answers such as 'we don't think much of it' are taboo. Valid arguments must be produced.

The second tier will consist of groups of three to six work units called work unit modules. Each team will be assigned an adviser (formerly such an official was known as a foreman). This adviser is the liaison officer between work units and specialists in the field of mechanics, sales, personnel policy, etc. The advisers must also channel information back to the work unit modules from the business unit. This team leads the production and includes the factory director (for whom a new title must be coined) and a high trade union official.

The fourth tier, the production advisory board, is responsible for the entire plant. This board will be composed of trade union officials, GM directors and members of the business units. Together they must reach consensus about such matters as salaries (including those of the directors) and profit-sharing. They report to the fifth tier: the strategic advisory board. This board is composed of a high trade union official plus the president of Saturn and his staff. Their task is long-term policy. Just as in the other four groups, decisions must always be reached by consensus.

4. There are often structural obstacles on the road to consensus. Employees are 'stimulated' to become experts with rigid preferences. This is encouraged by specialized education and training and even more by a narrow career pattern in which a person climbs one particular ladder in the organization. Obviously, more horizontal mobility can help prevent this. Another manner is purposely keeping the lines between tasks and specializations vague, thus preventing employees from taking only a narrow view. Overlapping responsibilities stimulate a broader perspective.

In addition to these structural measures, intervening directly in the *organizational culture* can be considered. This requires developing certain skills and a certain mentality. For instance, with regard to the fourth point, some companies very consciously promote a 'helicopter view'.

An important skill in the field of leadership has become known as 'management by walking around' (sometimes called 'management by wandering around'). Such managers seek communication and informal personal relations with their subordinates in a great many ways; they make themselves available, both at work and at after-hours' activities; many formal barriers and 'privileges'—for example, separate canteens—are eliminated. They welcome suggestions and ideas, and elicit reactions to their own ideas. In short, rather than being a hard-nosed decision-maker, such a manager becomes more of a coach and counsellor in the decision-making process; his goal is collective acceptance and consensus. The importance of this skill has been confirmed by numerous authors. The title of a recent article in the *Harvard Business Review* is illustrative: 'Good managers don't make policy decisions.' In this article, Wrapp (1984) stated that skilled managers only push decisions through in exceptional cases: 'They explore, combine and integrate!' Peters and Waterman (1982) also emphasized the importance of this skill in their book, *In Search of Excellence*. As an alternative title, they even considered 'Management by Walking Around'. A later work by Peters and Austin (1985) was devoted to this, in their view the most fundamental, skill.

In conclusion, it is interesting to hear what some Western managers who have spent several years in Japanese companies have to say:

A person who is a good leader in Japan does not make decisions at all—he finds out what the decision is. . . . And because you do not have specialists in Japanese companies, people tend to be more hesitant to make flat-out decisions. . . . If the president went ahead without the approval of the groups concerned, he'd be removed in some face-saving way (*Fortune*, 1982, p. 116).

According to Ouchi (1981), Japanese business culture utilizes numerous other skills in the process of consensus formation. People take more time to digest ideas. Ouchi calls this 'acceptance time'. Opinions tend to be more tentative and open-ended, rather than firm and unshakeable. People in general express themselves more delicately and subtly. This makes it easier to keep a decision-making process going, to keep trying out new ideas. Greater care can be taken in building up sufficient support and acceptance.

All the structural and cultural interventions described here have a common trait: they express a *greater interdependency* between management and employees.

Negotiating aspect

This aspect involves the tension balance between self-interests—trying to increase one's own share in the available resources—and the common interest of making the amount of resources available as large as possible. A certain amount of friction over scarce resources such as employee salaries, investment funds, and other tangible facilities is inevitable in organizations.

Measures to encourage organizational units to increase their share of the cake basically link a unit's performance to the resources available to it. Some ways of achieving this are:

- Develop transfer pricing arrangements for goods and services supplied by units in the organization. Allow units to buy these goods and services externally as well.
- Staff departments may offer their services on the open market.
- Allow units to retain a share of their profits for investment purposes.
- Allow units a bonus in proportion to their results.
- Link salaries to performance; give symbolic rewards.

In the above examples, resources are allocated proportionate to past results. Units acquire even greater freedom if resources are allocated with a view to *future* achievements. For instance, a unit's investment plans are evaluated along very general lines, or units can obtain venture capital relatively easily.

The generous allocation of resources often also implies a strong tendency to terminate losing operations. Unit managers are thus confronted with the consequences of their plans: their fate lies in their own hands. In fact, this refutes the portfolio strategy well known in consultancy circles, in which certain organizational units are milked by transferring their resources to promising units or 'stars'. As Pascale and Athos (1981, p. 57) so rightly stated: 'The principal fallacy of the portfolio concept is that all that frequently stands between a division being viewed as a cash cow or a star is management's creativity in seeing how to reposition their products in tune with the marketplace.'

Interventions such as these create productive tension and an entrepreneurial climate within units, while benefiting the organization as a whole. They comprise a paradoxical mixture of 'Take as much as you want for your own unit, but make sure it contributes to the whole!' They are easiest to implement if units have an autonomous product/market responsibility. It is much more difficult if the structure is highly functional.

Clearly, the interventions described thus far in this chapter supplement and reinforce one another. They cast *the highest echelon* in an organization in a different role as well. Its task becomes control and co-ordination *along general lines*; externally, its concern is the environment and related strategic issues. *Internally, the top management must create the conditions in which optimal productive tension can be achieved; it tries to maintain a certain equilibrium between units by adjusting the structure when necessary. External challenges and opportunities may also mean adapting the structure. If necessary, it acts as a platform for working out solutions to strategic questions and for resolving the inevitable frictions together with the unit managers, for example, if two units intend to market the same type of product. Finally, the larger whole acts as a safety net for managers and units that are willing to take risks.*

Socio-emotional aspect

This aspect involves the tension balance between a unit's need for an identity of its own and the backing of a small group, vs the emotional support of a larger whole. Pascale and Athos (1981) called the collective identity and the 'we-feeling' of certain large concerns 'the most underpublicized weapon of great companies'.

A strong 'we-feeling' can be developed by fostering common values. Several large companies have set down their goals and their mission in a sort of creed. They go to great lengths to gain acceptance for this creed among their employees. This can be accomplished in several ways:

- a colourful company history, perhaps in the form of 'sagas' from the pioneer days;
- the company's important societal role;
- its 'revolutionary' research and development;
- its more than superior service to its customers;
- its extensive investments in the education and training of its personnel;
- the exceptional quality of its products.

It should be possible for every organization to find a few characteristics along these lines on which to base an identity, a company pride. This identity can be strengthened in many ways:

- in a house style;
- by repeating the message at training activities, on buttons and posters, in annual speeches and at other official occasions;
- by selecting a 'suitable' type of employee.

When we set down a creed or express a shared identity in a house style, for instance, we anchor it in the structure. Basically, this implies an unremitting confirmation and articulation of the organization's values. It goes much further than merely chanting some mottoes and slogans. It is a way for oganizations to fulfil the emotional needs of their employees. We sometimes feel a little hesitant about this—is it not a dubious sort of indoctrination? Large Japanese companies certainly do not feel such scruples; many Western organizations as well have started developing the strong tie of shared values. Significantly, Peters and Waterman (1982), in their well-known study about excellent organizations, ascribed a central place to common values. They described seven levers for success: the 7S model. At the heart of this model is the S for 'Shared Values'!

Another way of strengthening the 'we-feeling' of the organization as a whole is to make the competition with other organizations more manifest. Continuous information about the company's results and products in comparison to those of the competitors is a powerful impulse.

Both of these mechanisms can also be applied within an organization to develop the identities of smaller units. Yet another device is the 'informalization' of relations within units. Informal relations with leeway for personal feelings can create close ties. Managements by walking around and contacts after working hours can contribute to this. It is even sometimes possible to create an informal atmosphere at the level of the organization as a whole.

Summary of change strategy: goals

We have seen that there are many ways of influencing the tension balance 'autonomy–interdependency'. Each of the other three relational aspects may contribute to it. We have seen that the various manners supplement and overlap one another. Again and again, the central relational aspect 'autonomy–interdependency' makes its influence felt. At most, the three other relational aspects give a certain emphasis. We have also seen that both the structure and the culture of the organization offer points of entry for achieving an optimal tension balance. (See the box 'What are the aims of organizational change?')

What are the aims of organizational change?

Structural changes
- distinct units with their own products
- relatively high degree of autonomy, responsibility for results
- direct feedback and exchange of results

Cultural changes
- MBWA, informal atmosphere, team development
- strengthening collective identity/shared values
- encouraging initiative/internal entrepreneurship

IN ESSENCE, IT MEANS
- *excelling and helping one another*

- *centralized and decentralized*
- *entrepreneurship and solidarity*

In practice, developing an optimal balance takes several years of continual effort and attention. Usually it is a process of trial and error in which managers attempt to achieve an effective level of productive tension, sometimes intuitively, by taking measures of their own, sometimes by borrowing from successful competitors. It is important to keep in mind a strategic point of view of the *direction* of organizational change in the sense described here. It gives an outline, a pattern, in which smaller changes can fit. It provides a perspective in which the proper choices can be made. Table 3.1 gives several examples of the choices and changes discussed. It shows both interventions to strengthen autonomy and interventions to strengthen interdependency.

What it is really about is a well-conceived organizational form. *The crux of the matter is that hierarchical steering and control are largely replaced by horizontal exchange and comparison. Results* of units are *made more visible* and *reported back more quickly.* This continual feedback of results and effects mobilizes energy. The rivalry with competitors is the external impulse, the rivalry to do well in comparison with other units the internal impulse to improve results. Relatively small and autonomous units influence one another much more effectively by means of regular mutual exchange and comparison than management possibly could. Such influence aims at results rather than functional prerogatives. In this way, competitive energy can be directly applied to achieving greater joint effectiveness. Staff departments, too, can develop in this direction, by setting up transfer pricing agreements for their services and/or giving them an opportunity to offer their services on the free market.

Table 3.1   The tension balance between autonomy and interdependency: examples of how to strengthen this balance

Autonomy	Interdependency
Profit centres with a high degree of independence as to: • internal structure • investments • product development • market strategy	Company facilities in fields such as: • research • risk capital • management development • scarce expertise
A more horizontal organization	Horizontal job rotation
Encourage initiatives/experiments	Clearly defined mission, 'we-feeling', house style.
Develop a unit-identity, informal climate, managing by walking around	Safety net for managers who take risk
Continual feedback and comparison of results	Increasing effectiveness by exchanging results and learning from one another
Our unit vs other units	Our company vs the outside competition

To summarize: Strong incentives to a productive tension are:

1. making results *visible*;
2. regular *feedback*;
3. *comparison* (internal and external).

The tension will be the more productive the more manifest are interdependency and a shared identity. This is where (3) *comparison* can become a highly productive learning experience to all involved.

A final remark on change strategy: goals

This discussion may give rise to the question why the management of an organization would want to introduce such far-reaching changes. In our 'political' view of organizations, the willingness to make such changes will increase as management discovers it can thus strengthen its own position. Internally, there is a great deal at stake: these changes mean risking established positions and decreasing the power distances. Externally, the matter is a different one. Pressure from the competition sometimes exacts large-scale internal adjustments to increase productivity. The pressure of increasingly scarce resources and the need for a more integral approach to problems may force government organizations in this same direction.

In my view, this is one more confirmation of the usefulness of a 'political' perspective of organizations. Maintaining and strengthening one's position are important incentives for adapting management and organization. If an organization is to keep pace with the competition in business and industry (in government organizations: the competition for increasingly scarce resources), then it cannot shy away from drastic changes. The recent disintegration of a few large conglomerates in the Netherlands has made a great impression. Smaller companies, too, can get into difficulties through internal rigidity and lack of motivation. The moral is clear: complicated dependency relations should be restructured in small, flexible market-oriented units. If we manage to combine this with strong incentives towards mutual exchange and support, we will contribute to more vital and competitive organizations.

The direction of change in organizations advocated in this chapter is closely related to the 'parties in a system' model described in Chapter 2. We have seen that the same categories—structure, culture and four types of tension balances—are basic to the strategy of change. Both party and system characteristics can be strengthened by articulating the tension balance between units; structure and culture both provide possible points of entry. Interestingly, this view can accommodate many of the management and organizational principles to be found in the literature on successful and excellent organizations (Grove, 1983; Kanter, 1983; Kilmann *et al.*, 1985; Ouchi, 1981; Pascale and Athos, 1981; Peters and Waterman, 1982; Peters and Austin, 1985).

3.3   CHANGE STRATEGY: APPROACH

In organizational change, consulting starts at the moment that the organization approaches a consultant with a problem or question. In the first analysis, the following two factors are important:

1. How extensive is the problem?
2. Can sufficient support be mobilized to solve the problem?

In answering the first question, it is important from what angle the problem is portrayed to the consultant. A problem can be defined in several ways, depending on the power positions and the specific interests of those involved. To find out the nature of the problem, the consultant may ask for an opportunity to seek more contacts in the organization, to carry out a preliminary study, or to set up an exploratory phase in the consulting project.

In answering the second question, he draws a 'political map': he localizes the positions in the organization which are of strategic importance in the decision-making about the problem (which he may or may not have reformulated). Then he investigates whether relations exist or can be developed between the various power centres to facilitate decisions, or to ensure that decisions will be made.

We must see both factors in relation to the network model of organizations as described in this book, in which the power and dependency relations between units are of central importance. The way units define the problem to consultants cannot be separated from their power positions (Chapter 4 will go into this in detail). For the second factor, the network model means that changes can only be effected in organizations if a foothold can be found for them. This implies that a heightened sensitivity to the 'political' structure is needed to achieve a solution. Here the consultant faces the question: can a combination of forces be found or developed with sufficient powers of decision to arrive at a solution?

3. A third factor is important. We must distinguish two levels of consulting. Here we need to recall our typology of relational aspects as described in the 'one-on-three model'.

    The 'one-on-three' model can be applied at two levels. We must distinguish between the conditioning and the operational level of organizational change. The conditioning level is the strategic level, at which the proper conditions are created in the organization for the achievement of the goals. The emphasis here is on power and dependency relations and on influencing them by way of the structure and the culture. The operational level is the level of specific problems in a limited number of units. The two levels emphasize different aspects of the problem area and interventions. The conditioning level looks to the 'architecture' of the organization; the operational level focuses more on repairs, maintenance and improvement. The basis the 'one-on-three' model provides at the conditioning level has been described in Section 3.2. The box 'Influencing organizational culture' gives an example of how this might be put into practice.

Influencing organizational culture

The top management of a company wanted to improve results by developing motivation and involvement. They exchanged views with a consultant about how this might be accomplished. In a preliminary orientation it was agreed that the consultant would present a list of 'levers to influence the company culture'. An abridged list follows below:

Levers to influence culture:
1. Directly, via the organizational culture:
   * house style;
   * company creed, identity, mission;
   * informal atmosphere;
   * investing in people: facilities/education and training;
   * symbolic rewards;
   * moral standards: *this* is how our company operates;
   * style of leadership, MBWA;
   * social skills, constructive meeting/negotiating;
   * internal entrepreneurship, incentives to experiment.
2. Via the 'detour' of the organizational structure:
   * decentralization/independent units;
   * units with integral products;
   * clear output criteria;
   * direct feedback of results;
   * units function as 'profit centres';
   * horizontal job rotation;
   * income depends on results;
   * systematic horizontal exchange of results.

The list was discussed at length. The intent was: (1) to come to a common view of the general direction in which the organization should develop; (2) to choose a limited number of levers—the most easily attainable!—to achieve this vision. The board chose to set down a company identity and a mission. Several talks led to a provisional formulation which was presented to the second echelon and the works council. Their suggestions were included in the definitive version. A plan of action was drawn up to propagate the mission in the company.

Later a second lever was selected: systematic horizontal exchange of results at different levels in the organization, under the motto of 'Sharing is learning'. A period of more than three years turned out to be necessary to get this going! It set in motion a drive for internal entrepreneurship.

The 'one-on-three' model also provides the necessary foothold at the operational level. The consultant is certainly not always expected to change structural and cultural conditions. More often he must deal with smaller-scale problems. In the following chapters we will see that the model can accommodate many specific problems. The framework applied to the problems in an organization is that of the relational aspects, each of which has corresponding 'malfunctions' and interventions. Interventions are aimed at clearing up or regulating 'malfunctions'. Examples of problems in the relations between units are: frictions in the co-ordination of tasks, personal irritations, deadlocks in allocating the available resources. We will become acquainted with the interventions appropriate to the various types of problems. The more chronic and insoluble the problems that the consultant encounters, the more he will have to consider interventions directly aimed at the conditioning level. Examples: decentralization, making a steep hierarchy more horizontal, developing more autonomous units. This implies that the conditioning level of restructuring the organization can be reached via the 'detour' of solutions to concrete problems. Insight into the conditions that form the background to the problems is important, even when a consultant is not working at the conditioning level. It increases his understanding of the problem situation considerably.

To recapitulate: the two levels of consulting are linked to the 'one-on-three' model. By specifically influencing and changing the power and dependency relations (the 'one' in the model), we influence the conditions that determine the organization. This is the conditioning level of consulting. Working at the conditioning level in a large part of the organization or even the entire organization means that the conditioning level coincides with the policy or strategic level. The direction of change and a large number of interventions to achieve it were described in Section 3.2. The operational level involves solving more immediate and concrete problems, in which the power and dependency relations are hardly at issue; here the emphasis of the interventions lies on the other three relational aspects. Table 3.2 briefly indicates what

Table 3.2   The operational level of consulting

Relational aspects	Kinds of problems	Effective strategies	Interventions
Instrumental aspect	Problems in co-ordination and synchronization, quality errors	Rational/technical approach: problem analysis, more efficient meeting and decision-making behaviour, improve planning, clearer allocation of tasks	Teach techniques of problem analysis and decision-making, introduce better co-ordination and planning procedures
Negotiating aspect	Continuous deadlocks, application of more and more pressure by both sides	Recognize controversies, give and take	Suggest compromises, training in negotiating techniques, chair negotiations
Socio-emotional aspect	Lack of trust and acceptance, personal irritations, stereotyping	Express 'irrational' feelings and irritations, promote 'informal' communication, empathy	Make irritations and stereotypes open for discussion, training in open communication

sorts of problems are involved and what sorts of interventions we might consider.

Table 3.2 anticipates the extensive treatment of these relational aspects in Chapters 5 and 6. Chapter 7 will describe in detail how a consulting method can be put into practice at the operational level. This chapter has covered the conditioning level of consulting.

Summary of 'change strategy: approach'

This section has outlined a strategic approach to change, based on the network model of organizations as described in this book, that co-ordinates the interventions in the four relational aspects. The approach is summarized in Figure 3.3.

Step 1   Identifying the problem

Step 2   Developing 'political' support in the organization

Step 3   Solving the problem with interventions from the 'one-on-three' model

Figure 3.3   Approach

3.4 CONCLUSION

The reader may well have been led to think that this change strategy is primarily applicable to organizational change in business and industry. Some non-profit organizations and government organizations are going through a similar process. Incentives in this direction are:

- increased public and political pressure for effectiveness and efficiency;
- increasingly scarce resources;
- the manifest disadvantages of the bureaucratic struggle for competence.

Public sector organizations have recently shown growing interest in commercial organizational and management principles. Various instruments are now being developed. I have in mind elements such as self-management, contract management, target group policy and reporting effects. The building blocks of this approach can be stated in four questions:

- How clearly can clients/customers be pointed out?
- How clear are the questions clients/customers have?
- How clear are the products supplied?
- How clear are the results?

Simple questions but sometimes difficult to answer. The more a non-profit organization adopts a policy of finding clear-cut answers to these questions, the better the positive dynamics as described here can be generated. It is facilitated by structuring an organization in units which are integrally responsible for a specific 'market' of clients and/or target groups. It also helps if exchange and comparison with other units are possible.

These four questions can also be regarded as four criteria to assess the 'added value' of an organizational unit. It is sometimes difficult to define the 'added value' due to a lack of signals from the market. This is not insurmountable. Alternatives for the signals of price and market share are: a 'pay-as-you-use' principle, opinion/satisfaction polls, client panel, complaint analysis, shadow prices, panel of 'opinion leaders' and output measurement.

Developing a feedback system is essential. It is an alternative to market signals. An organization need not wait until it has developed a finely tuned instrument. 'Keep it simple' and 'Build further on what you have' are good rules of thumb.

Finally, it is interesting to see how some change strategies described in the literature are related to the strategy advocated here. The three change strategies of Chin and Benne (1969) are classic:

1. *Power/coercion strategy*. In applying this strategy, a manager calls on the authority his position as a director or boss gives him to force employees to accept changes. This strategy takes advantage of the dependency of the employees and the fact that a person who offers resistance severely restricts his right to self-determination or autonomy.
2. *Empirical/rational strategy*. This strategy uses reasonable arguments to convince the employees of the usefulness and the appropriateness of the change. It appeals to their common sense. This strategy tries to persuade people to adapt their opinions and views by taking a rational and logical approach to change and to propagate new insights and opinions which can accommodate the change.
3. *Normative/re-educative strategy*. This strategy appeals to the norms and values of the employees. By 're-educating' them, it tries to change existing values, norms and behavioural patterns in such a way that new views and behavioural forms amenable to the change come about. This strategy makes an appeal to the person of the employee, his self-image and his self-esteem. In other words, here the identity of the employee is at issue, and perhaps the identity of the organization where he works.

Another almost equally classic work by Zaltman and Duncan (1977) added to the three strategies of Chin and Benne a fourth one:

4. This strategy creates conditions to bring about change by creating material and other facilities. (It is also known as the facilitative strategy.) The employees are promised 'rewards' if they accept the changes. This strategy appeals to the considerations employees make in terms of costs and benefits: a person will benefit by accepting the changes.

Two aspects are striking in these strategies: (1) they concentrate fairly strongly on those implementing the changes and the employees who must carry them out. There is relatively little attention to the organization in the

Table 3.3   Four change strategies and the 'one-on-three' model

Type of change strategy	Strategic angle of approach	Corresponding relational aspect
1. Power/coercion strategy	Dependency/ autonomy	Power aspect
2. Empirical/rational strategy	Insight, rational view/preference	Instrumental aspect
3. Barter/reward strategy	Share in scarce resources	Negotiating aspect
4. Normative/re-educative strategy	Identity, norms and values	Socio-emotional aspect

sense of 'Which organizational problem calls for which strategy?' Precisely this side of the matter has had our attention here; (2) all four of them fit into the one-on-three' model used in this book. This is shown in Table 3.3. We may broadly state that each of the four basic strategies emphasizes a particular relational aspect. In other words, each basic strategy focuses on a certain aspect in the relations.*

* I am indebted to M. Palmen for working out this point of view.

4 Power Relations in Organizations

4.1 INTRODUCTION

This chapter will treat one particular aspect of relations: relations between people in terms of power and dependency. *Three patterns of power relations are distinguished which will be related to behavioural tendencies and to particular problems for which specific interventions may be applicable.** We will work with three prototypes:

1. *Equal vs equal*—parties have approximately equal power.
2. *High vs low*—there is a more powerful and a less powerful party.

3. *High vs middle vs low*—one powerful party, one less powerful party and one least powerful party.

Each of them will be discussed in detail below.

Power was explained in Chapter 2. A few points will be recapitulated here: power is the capacity to determine the behaviour of others. Power and dependency are closely related. The more dependent parties are on each other, the more power they can exercise over each other, in the sense that they will have to take each other into account. We should certainly not depict power and dependency relations merely in terms of a higher position in a hierarchy or the power to wield sanctions and rewards. Power and dependency relations may also be determined by greater knowledge, a more central position in the

---

* Approaches to power in the form of prototypes can be found in Pondy (1967) and Elias (1971). Pondy distinguished a 'bargaining model': parties are equally powerful; a 'bureaucratic model': one party is more powerful than the other; and a 'systems model': the parties are highly interdependent. Elias distinguished several game models including the oligarchic type and the democratic type.

network or by moral ascendancy. So we must not think of the prototypes only in terms of formal hierarchical structures. In finding the power balances between the various positions in such a network, allowance is made for all possible forms of power and dependency; the final balance determines the parties' positions.

What we have in mind here is the subjective perception of power and dependency. People perceive others as more powerful or less powerful than they are. They know they are dependent and they act accordingly. The prototypes are meant as compact expressions of common power relations and the way they are subjectively perceived. By this I mean that *people are well aware of the position they occupy in relation to others, and their objective is to keep their position as firm as possible.*

Power is by no means a vague concept for the members of an organization. They know very well on what surrounding positions they are more and less dependent and they know to what extent they are able to determine the behaviour of the persons who occupy them. These are the power relations we are concerned with, for they govern our daily actions. Much behaviour is an attempt to maintain or strengthen one's strategic position in terms of these power networks. These attempts generally do not turn into manifest conflicts. Because there is interdependency and a need for co-operation, most behaviour is cautious and circumspect. It is difficult to bring into focus, but its consequences are evident.

The aim of this chapter is to show how the three prototypes are associated with certain behavioural tendencies and with certain specific problems. After this we will enumerate what sorts of interventions are available to organizational consultants in dealing with these problems.

The framework of this chapter is as follows:

Equal vs equal (Section 4.2);
High vs low (Section 4.3);
High vs middle vs low (Section 4.4).

The three prototypes represent frequently occurring power and dependency relations. If we look at the degree of dependence between a party A and a party B, then we can imagine the relations as shown in Table 4.1. In 2 and 3 the dependency is asymmetrical. These relations are 'high vs low'. The dependency is symmetrical in 1 and 4. Both cases involve 'equal vs

Table 4.1   Possible dependency relations

		A's dependence on B	
		Low	High
B's dependence on A	Low	1. Low interdependency	2. One-sided dependency
	High	3. One-sided dependency	4. High interdependency

equal' situations. And yet they are different. We can regard (1) and (4) as opposite poles on a continuum of gradually increasing interdependency. What consequences this increase in dependency has for the behavioural tendencies of those involved and for the choice of interventions will be discussed in Section 4.2.

For each of the three prototypes we will discuss:

(a) the behavioural tendencies of the parties involved;
(2) central problems;
(c) possible interventions.

The chapter will be concluded by:

Summary (Section 4.5);
Consequences for consultants: two examples (Section 4.6).

4.2 EQUAL vs EQUAL

Behavioural tendencies and central problems

If the parties are *of approximately equal power*, there is an impulse towards gradually increasing competition. Blake and Mouton (1961) studied these types of situations, including the escalation to a power struggle.

Briefly summarized: within the parties a more closely knit organization and a more authoritarian chain of command arise; between-parties stereotyping in terms of superior vs inferior begins; similarities are played down, differences accentuated. The situation comes more and more to resemble a win–lose struggle in which each party strives to subjugate the other.

Blake, Schepard and Mouton (1964) found that this process could easily be set in motion in *management–trade union relations*, sometimes in *staff–line relations, between functionally related departments of a firm such as sales and production, between individual companies in a corporation, and between partners in a merger*. In their view, the tendency towards *win–lose struggles* is a booby-trap in which both parties suffer great damage. All these relationships show a certain degree of interdependency, which the authors do not specify (in general terms, we could place them in the area between (1) and (4) in Table 4.1).

The stronger the interdependency, the more the strategies of the parties tend towards *negotiation* or even *co-operation*. Walton and McKersie (1965) described the negotiating behaviour between trade unions and employers. Pondy (1967) defined relations between departments as negotiating when the sum of the resources claimed exceeded the total amount available. *Even though people do their utmost to disguise the negotiations in these situations as rational decision-making processes*, they legitimate their claims with appeals to the common interests of the organization. Wildavsky (1964) pointed out that this horizontal relational pattern and the accompanying negotiating behaviour was applicable to various government services.

The above authors (Blake and Mouton, 1961; Pondy, 1967) and others (Landsberger, 1961; Dalton, 1959; Walton, Dutton and Cafferty, 1969) showed that 'equal vs equal' networks struggle with a central problem: the inherent tendency to some sort of rivalry and to gradually sharper forms of competitive behaviour. The strength of this tendency and the ease with which the situation ascalates have to do with the degree of interdependency. It can start with innocent haggling over positions, tasks and authority and end in win–lose struggles aimed at eliminating the opposing party. It takes very little to activate behaviour aimed at strengthening one's position, particularly in situations where interdependency is not very strong. This sets the stage for a development that tends to ignore the common interest. Obtaining the lead in the covert struggle for competence is felt to be more important.

Pondy was probably referring to the same tendency when he said: 'The fundamental source of conflict in such a system arises out of the pressure toward suboptimization' (Pondy, 1967, p. 318). Pondy found that the conflicts between departments resulting from this tendency to suboptimization seldom or never manifested themselves in the form of violent or openly aggressive action. More likely was 'the adoption of a joint decision process characterized by bargaining rather than problem-solving'. Pondy (1967, p. 319) is referring to a hostile and aggressive form of negotiation which he says increases the risk of new conflicts about other issues. This *tendency to suboptimization* can be manifested and reinforced in a wide variety of problems.* I will mention five.

1. A very important problem is to arrive at a precise *division of tasks and responsibilities*. Wrangling between horizontally related departments about the task definition is a constantly recurring source of difficulties: departments tend to avoid taking responsibility for tasks that require much time and manpower, while, on the other hand, they claim responsibility for certain important matters. Related to this is the inevitable problem of *task co-ordination*. A horizontal work flow from one department to another always leads to poorer co-ordination. People tend to lay the blame for this on others.
2. Units with different functions develop *different objectives and interests*. Production departments prefer lengthy production periods of the same standard product, while sales departments tend to emphasize fast supply to good customers, if necessary with varying specifications. Staff units are in favour of change because it gives them an opportunity to prove their worth, while line management tends more to stability.
3. The *dependency on common resources*. Departments not only share space, manpower, budgets, etc., but also central services such as administration and materials. Some haggling about the resources is inevitable. This creates a tendency towards pushing for their 'own' services.

---

* Suboptimization is the tendency for the units in an organization to work at a level under their capacity because of frictions between them.

4. *Obstructions to communication*. They may be physical differences, such as separating walls and geographic distance, but they may be differences in mentality. This means neither party is informed of, or even interested in, the other's opinions and suggestions.
5. *Differences in prestige* of the work. Some activities receive acclaim both inside and outside the organization. Large projects yield more success and greater prestige than several smaller ones. Sometimes the success and the competitive position of the organization are more immediately and clearly bound up with the work in a certain department. It almost goes without saying that this may lead to wry faces.

Such problems are unavoidable in organizations. They stem directly from the principles of the division of labour and specialization. Grouping activities in certain departments and services brings built-in tensions and frictions along with it. Suboptimization and deteriorating relations must not be allowed to gain the upper hand.

The degree of interdependency

The chance of serious suboptimization is related to the degree of interdependency.* Sherif (1966) made very clear how an intervention that has direct consequences for the dependency relation between the parties can bring about entirely different behaviour: he placed two autonomous groups of youths in a competitive situation. The result was fierce struggles. The introduction of superordinate goals, tasks which yielded mutual benefits and which could only be carried out with the aid of the other party, altered the behaviour in the direction of constructive consultation and even a degree of integration.

By drastically increasing and making manifest the interdependency, something essential in the situation changed. So there is a relationship between the degree of dependency and probable forms of behaviour. The greater the *interdependency*, the less people can *afford conflicts*. Conflicts are more and more obviously in contrast to their own interests. This increases the chance of negotiating, sometimes even problem-solving and co-operative behaviour. In fact, the degree of interdependency is a more important factor than having *equal* power. The greater the interdependency, the more the *power* of the parties *over each other* increases. They are forced to take each other into account.

March and Simon (1958) stated that greater interdependency meant a greater urgency to come to joint decision-making. This does not imply that there is no longer any chance of a conflict. But its nature becomes more instrumental or socio-emotional. Elimination or subjugation of the opposing party becomes contrary to one's own interests.

The interdependency becomes very clear when loss for one party directly

* Here we are referring to the interdependency as subjectively perceived by the parties involved.

and manifestly means loss and disadvantage for the other, or if advantage for one automatically means advantage for the other. The more individual units are incorporated in a single identity with distinct common interests and goals, the less chance there is of suboptimization and escalation to a power struggle. The focus of interest is shifted to an even *better task co-ordination*, and to *the socio-emotional aspect* of preventing or openly discussing irritations and further developing the human potential. An important incentive to this is that everyone stands to gain when no one functions beneath his capacities and that removing obstacles, no matter in whose interests they were initially, is to everyone's benefit. In other words, in this situation as well many problems and conflicts may arise, but the damage that everyone will suffer and the necessity of finding solutions are much more evident.

We can express the degree of interdependency on a continuum in Figure 4.1. Relatively autonomous positions involve isolated units that are interdependent because they compete in the same 'space'. One position can always gain an advantage by eliminating the other position: winner takes all. Example: two companies that compete in the same market. Dependent autonomous positions refer to the interdependency of a zero-sum game: gain for one is loss for the other, but at the same time gain for one is only possible if the other position remains in existence. Example: the relationship between employers and employees.

Relatively autonomous positions	Dependent autonomous positions	Pooled interdependency	Sequential interdependency	Reciprocal interdependency	Synergetic interdependency

Increasing interdependency   ------➤

Figure 4.1   Types of interdependency

In order to conceptualize the following three types of interdependency, the distinction of Thompson (1964) into 'pooled', 'sequential' and 'reciprocal' is useful. With pooled interdependency, units have certain shared resources, for example a warehouse, administrative support or a training unit, but otherwise work independent of each other.

Sequential interdependency involves dependency in a time sequence; output for one is input for the other. In situations of reciprocal interdependency the work moves back and forth several times between units. This involves the highest degree of interdependency of these three.

Finally I distinguish synergetic interdependency as a type of interdependency in which explicit advantage for one automatically means advantage for the other, and where advantage can only be obtained through joint effort. Example: a research team.

What we are concerned with here is the relationship between the degree of

Degree of dependency ------>

Figure 4.2   Dependency and behavioural tendencies—1

interdependency and behavioural tendencies, which is expressed in Figure 4.2. These behavioural tendencies are discussed more fully in Chapter 5. Here we can summarize this behaviour as shown in Table 4.2.

Table 4.2   Dependency and behavioral tendencies—2

Characterization of the *behavioural tendencies* of the parties	*Power struggle.* If it is advantageous, false information is provided; one's own goals receive priority; no concessions unless as a means to a greater victory	*Negotiating.* One-sided information is given; goals are clung to as long as possible, but there is also room for concessions	*Co-operation.* Openness in information flow; openness about goals, which are accommodated in joint objectives
Desired result	*Subjugation* of opposing party	Favourable *compromise*	A high-quality *solution*. Mutual *understanding*

If the interdependency between the parties is relatively low, as it is on the left-hand side of the typology in Table 4.2, in principle the parties need not give much consideration to each other. But as soon as an element of competition for scarce goods or power positions starts to play a role, parties will readily tend to adopt strategies to subjugate the other. One's own interest soon comes to be defined in terms of eliminating the other or keeping him under control. In the right-hand columns of Table 4.2 are situations in which parties must look to each other to be able to work effectively *themselves*. Co-operative and helpful behaviour is in the direct interests of those involved in such a situation.

We can also view the probability with which certain problems will present themselves to those involved in relation to the degree of interdependency of the units. Figure 4.3 shows a general typology.

Characterization of possible problem definitions by parties	How do we put a stop to the struggle for competence/power?	How do we arrive at a fair division of scarce resources?	How do we achieve optimal co-ordination?

Degree of dependency ------>

Figure 4.3   Dependency and likely problems

Even under conditions of very high interdependency, frictions can escalate to win–lose struggles. It is the task of the consultant to find in the degree of dependency an indication of the feasibility of different interventions. He can set himself more realistic goals. At one extreme, for instance, he will endeavour to keep the parties as separate as possible, while at the other extreme he will organize intensive feedback sessions followed by elaborate discussions about task co-ordination.

Interventions

In equal vs equal relations the focus for interventions shifts along with the degree of interdependency. More to the right in Figure 4.3 we will meet task-oriented and socio-emotional interventions as elaborated in the organizational development literature. Around the centre we will find interventions to deal with allocation problems, such as increasing negotiating skills of those involved or having a central authority or even a consultant act as intermediary.

Further to the left, the problems are of a nature such that we will have to tackle the network itself: either separate the parties, or else make them much more dependent upon each other. Sometimes we will have to lean heavily on the central authority in order to find a solution.

These interventions can be classified into four groups:

1. *Changing the network itself.* For example:
   • clearly demarcate departments;
   • decentralize administration;
   • enlist liaison officers or efficiency experts for interface management;
   • bring departments more into balance in the case of asymmetries in status or knowledge by reallocating responsibility or by strengthening the 'weakest';
   • strengthen the role of a central authority on points such as enforcing rules, fixing demarcation lines, arbitration; if necessary, merge departments under one manager.
2. *Improving task co-ordination.* For example:
   • create a clearer task division;
   • group activities on the basis of reciprocal interdependencies (Thompson, 1964);
   • improve co-ordination procedures;
   • form buffer stocks to enable departments to make their own planning.
3. *Structuring negotiating.* For example:
   • arbitrate, have parties formulate their conditions for co-operation;
   • chair negotiations;
   • keep the rank and file at arm's length;
   • train parties in negotiating techniques.
4. *Improving interpersonal relations.* For example:
   • train parties in coping with conflict;

- set aside a regular time to discuss problems in relations and obstructions to mutual effectiveness;
- exchange personnel.

The predominately structural interventions under (1) attempt to change the potentially risky situation of relatively low interdependency.* Basically, there are two ways of doing this:

(a) Reducing interdependency so that neither party has any power over the other (for instance, separating the parties or having co-ordination decisions made by a higher echelon);
(b) Increasing interdependency so that disadvantage for one means disadvantage for the other (for instance, by assigning them a joint task or by integrating them into one entity).

The second way was discussed at length in Chapter 3. Here we will give a few more examples of possible interventions:

- Stimulate the 'we-feeling'. A colourful tradition, achievements that command prestige and respect from the environment, joint activities, comparison with the achievements of the previous year, the struggle against competitors, are all good ways of doing this.
- Provide for horizontal mobility. This creates managers with an overall outlook. It makes the web of dependencies more manifest and keeps internal rivalry mild. For next year one may have to manage a 'competing' department!
- Structure the organization in surveyable units with their own clear responsibilities (including profit if possible). These units should have an integral product of their own, and not merely a certain functional aspect or specialism. Often it is possible to integrate certain staff activities in such a unit.
- Give units opportunities to bring new products on the market themselves, and to influence their own incomes by linking them to achievements.

With these interventions we are working at the conditioning level. The interventions under (2), (3) and (4) are more immediate aids to operational problems. With a fairly large degree of dependency, especially when there is an adequately functioning central authority, interventions at a conditioning level are generally not the answer. Interventions focus more on the strategies parties adopt in dealing with each other and what effects they have. The object is to bring about a behavioural change so that the parties own interests as well as their interdependency come into better relief. Sometimes consultants try to find *ad hoc* solutions to the problems, for instance, in a better co-ordination procedure or a clearer task division.

---

* Risky because it is precisely here that the parties so readily define their own interests in terms of eliminating the other party.

Table 4.3   Different problem definitions and different focuses in approaching them, with from top to bottom: increasing interdependency

Examples of 'equal vs equal'	Examples of problems and behavioural tendencies	Examples of interventions
Separate firms in the same market	Sharp competition	Arbitration
Different ministries with tangent interests	Constant struggle for competence	Develop central authority/ motivate it to intervene
		Establish demarcation lines
Independent firms working on the same project	Negotiations bog down	Develop central authority/ motivate it to intervene
Partners in a merger	Constant bickering about the proper structure and the division of authority	Mediate
		Structure negotiations, perhaps as impartial chairman
Staff–line relationships	Covert fighting for positions	Establish negative effects of manner of working together: organizational mirroring, confrontation meeting
Relationships between functionally related departments and services	Insufficient co-ordination and synchronization	
	Delayed decision-making, poor co-operation	Develop better co-ordination procedures
	Irritated personal relations	Improve skills in negotiating and meeting

I would like to recapitulate these remarks in a diagram summarizing several examples. In Table 4.3, the left-hand column gives examples of equal vs equal situations, the next column lists problems and behavioural tendencies which may be considered manifestations of the move towards suboptimization and a power struggle. The examples are classed in three groups: from top to bottom according to increasing interdependency.

It seems fairly evident that the type of intervention will shift with the degree of interdependency. Apart from that, within organizations there are a few conditions and skills that are very helpful in preventing equal vs equal relations from deteriorating. Here we can primarily think of the concrete role of the central authority and of developing contacts and acceptance.

Important in tensions and conflicts between organizational units is a properly functioning *central authority*. It must be able to subject internal rivalries to rules and to intervene when the situation threatens to escalate. This central unit or person can define the interdependency or further increase it by assigning new joint tasks, it can encourage co-operative behaviour or punish hostile behaviour. A central authority can also make decisions in questions which seem likely to escalate, for example, if there is an acute shortage of resources. If the parties have no central authority above them, not allowing suboptimization to get the upper hand puts a great strain on them.

With many horizontal tensions in organizations, what is really most important is to keep obstacles in view and open for discussion. Schisms and escalation can best be avoided by continually monitoring tensions and incidents between departments. *Keeping in touch about these matters ensures that the necessary adjustments are made and* ad hoc *measures taken.* These are the regular contacts about a variety of matters with a variety of directly involved persons who must see to it that no permanent rifts occur between parties. It is important to prevent polarization from occurring, so that sufficient acceptance and goodwill among those involved are maintained for improvisation and accommodation. Tensions, differences of opinion and conflicts are a fact of life in equal vs equal networks. The trick is to retain control over the conflict inherent in these networks. Paradoxically, tensions and differences of opinion are very useful for this.

Coser (1964) stated that conflict makes the parties more highly involved with one another and that, unless relations have already deteriorated too far, it restores unity and stability to them. He found support for this in the experiences of Bach and Wijden (1969) and in the research results of Corwin (1969) which stated that with an increase in the number of small differences of opinion, the number of large clashes decreased.

Robbins (1974) considered it an important task of management to maintain a mild level of conflict. Being afraid to do this means allowing an important source of necessary adjustments and innovations to go to waste. Van de Vliert (1981a) even gave a systematic survey of the factors that can bring about some degree of escalation if needed.

Summary of equal vs equal

Horizontal balances of power between organizational units are somewhat unstable. Because of the impulses towards strengthening one's own position with respect to surrounding positions, disturbances in the balance of power can occur fairly easily. This sometimes gives rise to a tendency towards power struggles which it is difficult to control. If interdependency is not very strong matters can easily escalate further. Suboptimization—some of the production capacity of organization parts is lost because more and more energy is consumed by their bickering—is the result.

Depending on the degree of interdependency, the problems manifest themselves differently. The feasibility of various interventions also depends on it. For a broad 'intermediate area' of interdependency in which, for instance, we can locate relations between departments in organizations, the following statements provide a framework for interventions. It is important that:

1. A certain equilibrium is maintained between the parties;
2. There is an integrative potential in the form of a central authority or a strong common interest accepted by the parties;
3. There is clarity about task division and co-ordination;

4. The inevitable frictions are specified and 'spread out' (spreading over time, varying issues, varying parties and conditions, splitting up large issues into several smaller ones, translating matters of 'principle' into concrete terms, reducing what happened in the past to what is now still possible);
5. Skills in handling conflicts are developed; examples: confrontation and negotiation.

These points work preventively. Once the impulse towards a win–lose struggle has obtained the upper hand, we will have to consider more structural interventions, even if it is only temporarily: for instance, a stricter separation of parties or a greater influence of the top on certain matters.

4.3   HIGH vs LOW

Behavioural tendencies and central problems

The powerful vs less powerful network is sometimes referred to by such epithets as 'haves–have-nots'; 'topdogs–underdogs'; centre–periphery, 'establishment–outsiders'. There is a wealth of literature about the behavioural tendencies of the groups in such a network in very divergent social contexts. Interesting politicological, sociological and social psychological work has been performed as well (Deutsch, 1973; Elias, 1969; Elias and Scotson, 1977; Kipnis, 1972; Veblen, 1899; Michels, 1970). Based on the literature and his own experiments, Kipnis (1972) stated that powerful persons, compared to less powerful persons, tend to:

1. Accumulate further power, prestige, financial gain, etc.;
2. Feel they are above the less powerful;
3. Exploit and manipulate the less powerful.

It is remarkable how less powerful people often incorporate the low opinion more powerful persons have of them in their own self-images. Boekestijn (1979) accounted for this by the fact that it is risky to put up any resistance to the negative qualification of the more powerful. Rather than challenging more powerful persons, the less powerful accept the negative assessment the dominant group has of them in order to make themselves acceptable.

It is also remarkable how sensitive people are to changes in power relations. Elias (1969) in particular emphasized that emotional and behavioural tendencies are reinforced when people *acquire* greater or lesser power.

Table 4.4 is a very general summary of some tendencies of more powerful and less powerful persons in a 'high vs low' network.

This model of high/low relations is still too general. The behavioural tendencies and problems in hierarchical relations in organizations will have to be specified. A great deal of research has been performed on this question, although much of it was quite one-sided on the problems of leadership.

What are the problems of leadership? Kotter (1979) had an interesting

Table 4.4 Behavioural tendencies high vs low

High	Low
Overestimation of their own power; adopt an attitude of 'We don't need them, they need us.'	Apathy and subjugation, with intermittent but little effective outbursts of aggression
Little willingness to face up to developments which demand that relations be re-evaluated. 'We've done all we can.'	Even if the balance of power changes in their favour, their attitude is one of irresolution and hesitancy. Achieving good internal organization is often a long-drawn-out process. They often overestimate the rationality of the other party
Superior attitude: 'Why all the mistrust, we are well aware of our responsibilities.'	React to contact with the arrogant establishment with indignation and aggression
Tendency to derision, rigidifying into grimness. 'This is simply going too far, those blokes should be put in their place.'	Strengthening their own organization. Tendency to provocation and to militant action
Tunnel vision: 'We have their interests at heart, but there is no way to get through to them. If they don't want to listen, they will have to take the consequences.'	Tunnel vision: 'We can only make things any better by fighting. The entire system is rotten.'

view on this. He stated that as organizations become more complex, managers grow more and more dependent on others, especially on their subordinates. How can they retain control in the face of increasing dependency? By developing their power in a certain manner. In other words, by keeping their subordinates dependent after all. Kotter showed that *formal position* and *power of persuasion* are often not enough. Examples of other manners are: *obligating* people to them by granting them certain *favours*, or by showing that one *controls* a number of essential *resources such as money, information and relations*. In other words, what they can do is develop an arsenal of sanctions and rewards.

Pondy (1976) took a view similar to Kotter's, but he also incorporated in it the behaviour of subordinates. He felt the *central problem* in hierarchical relationships was attempts by superiors to get a better grip on those under them vs the endeavours of subordinates to maintain or to increase their autonomy. 'Vertical conflicts in an organization usually arise because superiors attempt to control the behaviour of subordinates, and subordinates resist such control' (Pondy, 1967, p. 314).

Pondy classified these attempts by superiors into two groups:

1. *Replacing personal power by impersonal power.* Better rules and procedures, more precise task definitions, establishing routines;
2. *Changing the manner of exercising power. Different leadership style*, one which makes more use of persuasive and participative methods.

Swingle (1976) described more extensively how the top of an organization maintains its position. A wide variety of mechanisms are used. Examples are:

1. Tying up complaints or proposals from subordinates in bureaucracy and red tape;
2. Setting up complicated and clumsy participation procedures to create the illusion that subordinates really do have influence;
3. Stigmatizing and isolating resistance, if necessary eliminating it: some people do not see it this way → they lack a sense of responsibility → they are agitators and troublemakers → they must be eliminated!

Swingle is quite fervent as well as rather biased about what he calls 'bureaucratic strangulation'. He identifies with the perceptions of 'low' and this makes his view interesting.

How do subordinates protect their *autonomy*? Because the relationship is hierarchical, they must use *subtle strategies*. Open resistance is generally too risky. Examples are:

- withholding information;
- keeping agreements vague;
- carefully defining their own territory;
- passive resistance;
- solidarity with colleagues;
- making themselves indispensable in a particular area;
- evading control;
- endless delays.

Table 4.5 summarizes what positions the parties tend to take with respect to the classic problems of 'resistance to change', just one expression of the central problem of 'control vs autonomy'. Another frequent expression is known as the 'motivation problem'—'How do we motivate our employees?'

Clearly, hierarchical regulation and control can become very costly for organizations. Enthusiasm, willingness to adapt, concern for the product and a spirit of enterprise are traits which can become very scarce in the lower echelons of the organization.

Interventions

Below we will describe how consultants sometimes deal with high vs low relations. Different ways will be distinguished: formalizing power relations,

Table 4.5   Control vs autonomy

	High	Low
Central problems	How can we keep things under *control*? How do we get across what has to be done? How can prove it is fair? How do we promote acceptance? What will we do about resistance? How can we find out what people think?	How do we avoid being taken in? Committing ourselves to things we do not want? Can you really speak your mind freely; won't they get back at you later? Is the matter still open; do we really have all the information? Will we be called obstructionists?
Image of the other	Inflexible, suspicious. Not very creative: 'Nothing will come of it.' Think only of their own interests: 'They don't give a hang about the company.'	Manipulating, calculating: 'They'll have it their way after all.' 'They know more than they tell you.' 'They always think of themselves first.'
Examples of strategies	Setting down consultation procedures. Influencing opinion leaders. Reasoning. Coercion: 'You can't please everyone.'	Refusing to take active part, withholding information, concealing their opinions. 'Let them first say what it is they are after.' Scepticism. Passive attitude. Find a safe haven for their interests (representatives in the works council or trade unions)

personalizing power, the organizational development approach and finally a fourth way.

Formalizing power relations

Pondy (1967) stated that personal power can be replaced by impersonal mechanisms, such as procedures and systems, to improve control over the behaviour of subordinates. Other authors also found that formalization of power was a common means of control (Meyer, 1972; Pfeffer, 1978). By giving a few examples, we will take a closer look at this concept below.

Taylor's contribution to organizational science fits well into our context of tensions between superiors and subordinates. His methods were largely intended for obtaining a better grasp on the activities of subordinates, something which was sorely needed as far as Taylor was concerned. He gave many descriptions of how employees managed to restrict production. He saw the cause of this 'soldiering or loafing' not so much in a sort of inborn tendency to laziness as in 'second thought and reasoning caused by their relations with other men' (Taylor, 1947, pp. 19–24).

He repeatedly stated that his 'scientific method' using individual training, separation, special reward systems and other measures could gradually transcend the pressure of colleagues and thus combat output restrictions (Taylor, 1947, pp. 32, 34, 69, 72–4). Taylor vividly described his experiences as a foreman in a steelworks:

> As was usual then, and in fact as is still usual in most of the shops in this country. The shop was really run by the workmen, and not by the bosses. The workmen together had carefully planned just how fast each job should be done, and they had set a pace for each machine throughout the shop, which was limited to about one-third of a good day's work. Every new workman who came into the shop was told at once by the other men exactly how much of each kind of work he was to do and unless he obeyed these instructions he was sure before long to be driven out of the place by the men (Taylor, 1947, pp. 48–9).

Taylor fought for three years to break this system of agreements.

> No one who has not had this experience can have an idea of the bitterness which is gradually developed in such a struggle. . . . And there are few foremen indeed who were able to stand up against the combined pressure of all the men in the shop. . . . If the writer had been one of the workmen, and had lived where they lived, they would have brought such social pressure to bear upon him that it would have been impossible to have stood out against them (Taylor, 1947, pp. 50–1).

From these tumultuous experiences Taylor distilled, as he called it, his 'scientific management' (Taylor, 1947, pp. 52–3).

This case gives a good idea of how personal power can be replaced by 'neutral' mechanisms and also of the tremendous pressure which is elicited when autonomy is undermined. (Incidentally, when we read what Taylor wrote, it is rather amazing that the discovery of the primary group and the informal organization is ascribed to Mayo *et al.*)

Despite the strong resistance Taylor encountered, his methods were introduced on a large scale, clearly because of the existing surplus of power on the part of management. Taylor's own intentions were entirely different. He believed that the interests of employers and workers were essentially the same. 'The great mental revolution which occurs under scientific management' would do away with contention and antagonism and replace them by 'friendly co-operation and mutual helpfulness'. The dream of an idealist? Taylor met with quite some contention and antagonism in his experiences. It was also the time of the rise of the unions, when sharp and often bloody conflicts were the order of the day.

The 'friendly co-operation and mutual helpfulness' never really materialized, seeing that management simply ignored the changes demanded of themselves. 'Nine-tenths of our trouble has been to "bring" those on the management's side to do their fair share of the work and only one-tenth of our trouble has come on workmen's side' (Taylor, 1947, p. 43).

Another striking example of how power relations can interfere in the efforts of experts or consultants can be found in the relationship between technology and organization. Many organizational sociologists regard technology as an important explanatory factor of organization. The fact that workers man an assembly line, that their work on that line has been reduced to relatively simple repetitive actions, need not be considered a sort of law which technology has imply thrust upon us.

Parallel to Taylor's methods, using technology to break the work down into simple routines means that people without too much education and motivation can be enlisted. This keeps management independent of the goodwill of task performers. The work is relatively easy to control. If a worker gets out of hand, it is easy to find a replacement. It is also easy to follow economic cycles. If production drops it is easy to fire people, for little has been invested in them. If the demand rises, then more workers are hired and they can start immediately. When workers do not have a position protected by legislation or by strong trade unions, a hire-and-fire policy is perfectly normal. If it is not so easy to fire personnel, if one is faced with the necessity of finding and motivating expensively trained workers, if the labour market is tight for some length of time, then one turns to task expansion, work structuring, group tasks and such. Suddenly the technology offers plenty of elbow-room.

The technology is not the determining factor when factory managers adopt such systems. Nor is it merely a question of having a surplus of power, or attempting to maintain or to increase it. A primary factor is definitely the *competition with other companies*. In order to maintain one's position in the market, one is actually *forced* to exploit the subordinate position of the lower echelons. Environmental conditions can also make one dependent on the efforts and the creativity of the lower echelons. Then one will also have to give expression to the greater mutual dependency in the structure and culture of the organization in order to compete successfully (see Chapter 3).

These examples illustrate the *depersonalization of power distances* through the introduction of a wide variety of 'neutral' techniques and procedures in the context of the competition between companies. These techniques and procedures become the formal rules and given structures to which people have to adapt. Consultants should keep in mind possible side-effects of some of these measures: bureaucratization and growing demotivation. A transport organization is quite likely to decrease feelings of powerlessness and frustration for many employees.

Personalizing power

Another way of dealing with high vs low relations is personalizing power. We will concentrate on the *style of leadership*. We will regard the behaviour of subordinates as being determined by *the style* of leadership. McGregor (1960) is a prominent *example*.

McGregor cast his view of the determining role of the style of leadership in the form of a self-fulfilling prophecy. If a boss assumes that an employee is lazy, that he shows no initiative and lacks a sense of responsibility, that only financial inducements can motivate him to some sort of achievement, then a boss will constantly keep his eye on him, tell him precisely what he should and should not do, perhaps set down a policy of monetary sanctions, but he will take an indifferent attitude towards other working conditions. Unfortunately, the employee will conduct himself in a hostile manner, will be lax, will do nothing when his boss is not there, enjoy it when things go wrong, and so on. Exactly what his boss expects of him.

There is logic to this. Still, McGregor picks out one characteristic of the high vs low situation: the image high has of low. It is a characteristic which can also be seen as a result of the high–low difference, but which McGregor sees as the cause. Like this, he relegates to the background very important elements of power and leadership such as decisions about promotions and dismissals, about incomes and appraisals, about retaining or giving up certain tasks, about a wide variety of positive and negative sanctions which may instil employees with strong feelings of dependency.

Even if we could manage to cover up the power differences behind this with a congenial participative style, then it would still be the question whether subordinates would really react very differently. Are they not more likely to wonder what will happen in a concrete situation, when opinions and interests clash? If the more powerful party turns out to have the deciding voice after all—and why not—then their behaviour will be guarded with a view to their own interests, especially if 'repercussions' (not to say retaliations) seem likely.

Another objection to the personalization of power is that it suggests that a different way of dealing with power is primarily a matter of personal discrimination of individual managers. In my view the *feasibility of changing the style*, despite the will to do so and despite support and training, *can be limited by several strong conditions*. In the first place, as long as superiors have an arsenal of sanctions and rewards at their disposal and are prepared to use it, this will continue to influence the behaviour of subordinates.

In the second place, managers are generally in some sort of competitive situation with other managers; in their turn, they try to acquire autonomy and influence with respect to their superiors. This often means a tendency towards more goal-oriented and relatively 'firm' leadership.

Summarizing: we are dealing with a dynamic equilibrium of a great many forms of dependency. Changing one element ('style of leadership') may perhaps bring about a different equilibrium, but if other more structural matters do not change as well, the effect will be slight.

The style of leadership is very evidently the central variable in much of the management and organizational literature. Changing the style of leadership by means of an elaborate and lengthy programme is the crux of some intervention strategies. Is this nonsense in view of the above? Not in cases where there is a discrepancy between the style of leadership and actual interdependency. For instance, in a situation of great dependency on the expertise of subordinates, in the case of absence of sanctions and rewards because they are in the hands of higher managers or other officials such as the personnel manager. This approach can be useful for adapting the behaviour of managers to such changed relationships, especially when other conditions relating to organizational structure and culture have also been changed, as was elaborated in Chapter 3. Concentrating on these conditions is another way in which consultants can deal with power differences.

The structural approach

Organizational development pays a great deal of attention to such matters as *human relations, participation, work structuring and group tasks*. This is a somewhat broader approach than a change of management style. In recent years this approach has been supplemented with specific views about successful and excellent organizations. One of these authors, Ouchi (1981), established a direct link to organizational development. He mentioned many similarities and recommended OD as a way of accomplishing organizational adaptation and developing 'interpersonal skills'. Some of his success cases of 'theory Z' organizations, such as the efforts of Likert in a General Motors factory, could have come straight from a handbook on organizational development. We also see these kinds of recommendations from other quarters. Various authors closely affiliated with the McKinsey group emphasized that more attention should be paid to the 'soft' side of organizations: climate, skills, style of leadership, shared values, concern for the development of personnel are the keys to success.

We summarize this approach below with a few examples. (For a more complete discussion see Chapter 3.)

1. *Structural adjustments*, such as:
   - making the organization more horizontal;
   - delegating responsibilities, for instance, assigning self-contained tasks to groups, including such tasks as quality control and planning;
   - bringing the staff closer to line management.
2. *Cultural adjustments*, for instance, changes in *leadership style*. Important elements in a style to reduce tensions are:
   - coaching and counselling;
   - striving for consensus;
   - skills in mediating and bridging gaps;
   - striving for good informal interpersonal relations;
   - being present and available at the place of work;
   - willingness to experiment;
   - providing opportunities for employees to develop their capacities.

So this approach involves changes that influence interdependencies on a large scale. It also takes advantage of structural changes towards more democratic relations which are in progress. These are changes that already have a good foothold in the organization and in society.

A fourth approach

Especially in specific situations of deteriorating relations between haves and have-nots in communities, we need other types of interventions. These interventions can also be of great value when tensions occur along the hierarchy in organizations. In order to avoid the pitfall of stereotyping and gradual escalation and polarization, Deutsch (1973) worked out an *alternative* for the 'have-nots'. He felt this approach would decrease the chances of a ruinous conflict for both parties and maximize the chances of concrete results for the 'have-nots'.

Deutsch recommended the following strategy for the 'have-nots':

1. Make clear and specific proposals for change;
2. Pay attention to the problems and costs the 'haves' will face if they go along with the proposals; show explicit willingness to tackle these problems together with the 'haves' and to keep the costs as low as possible.
3. Clarify the advantages for the 'haves' of reaching such an agreement. For example, improvement of the reputation and goodwill of the 'haves'; fewer internal problems;
4. Clarify the consequences of not reaching a compromise;
5. Show the effort, power and resolution of the 'have-nots' to change the situation; if the 'haves' do not give this any credence, a carefully executed action showing what kind of organization and other potential power sources the 'have-nots' can mobilize can be effective.

Nor is it difficult to mention behavioural alternatives for the 'haves'. A few points seem important to me:

1. Being sensitive to the changes which have taken place in the network of power and dependency relations of which they are a part, rather than clinging unconditionally to their own positions;
2. Knowing the backgrounds of the other party's behaviour. Not only the business aspects, but also the underlying images and feelings;
3. Having some notion of the dynamics of the situation: the chance of escalation and its consequences;
4. Taking an explorative attitude: what exactly do they want, followed by negotiating with concretely worked out proposals and counterproposals.

It is not easy to bring this into practice, but working along these lines helps draw the contours of this approach, an approach that makes ample use of our insights into high–low relations. Is such an approach easy to learn and to convey?

The following revealing example is taken from Oshry's 'power and systems training'. Participants in a conference are physically put in the situation of 'establishment vs outsiders'. Some of the participants are given luxurious accommodation with every convenience, as well as control of the kitchen, electricity, hot and cold water and means of communication with the outside world; the others must get along with a minimum of means and have little control. Oshry sometimes does this with representatives of real establishment–outsider configurations, and has them change roles. The dynamics of the situation turn out to be so strong that after a while the representatives of the establishment (but now in the role of 'outsiders') 'spontaneously' take to vindictive and apathetic or aggressive and unreasonable behaviour. The representatives of the outsiders, on the other hand, have no difficulty assuming their role as 'establishment', adopt a self-complacent attitude and allow the others to share in their prosperity only sparingly. During the training it is just as hard to keep the parties from falling into the trap of a destructive conflict as it normally is. This is much more than a cognitive experience. It can lead to an understanding of the 'unreasonable' behaviour of the other party and can make people aware of the how the conflict might be handled.

Power relations are sensitive, and one of the parties will readily regard any changes in them as unwanted. In an 'equal vs equal' situation, structural solutions are more or less expected of the consultant, as long as a certain balance continues to exist. In a 'high vs low' situation tinkering with the network may be perceived as taking sides, which poses a threat and mobilizes great resistance. *Except if the power and dependency relations are already clearly changing and if there are serious tensions and conflicts.* I see some perspective in a clarification of the emotional and behavioural consequences of the high–low relationship and of the pitfalls inherent in it along with some structural changes.

Summary of high vs low

We started by summing up the characteristics of 'high vs low' networks. Examples: high wants control, low wants autonomy; high senses resistance to change, low feels it is being manipulated. The dynamics of such a network can lead to a few pitfalls: increasing arrogance vs apathy or aggression, for instance. Four types of interventions consultants might use were discussed:

1. Replace personal power by impersonal power. For example: by establishing production routines, creating a system of rules and procedures for personnel and organization policy.
2. Change the style of wielding power. For example: training that alters the style of leadership, creating teamwork, changing managerial attitudes.
3. The organization development approach. For example: task structuring, decentralization.
4. Developing insights into, and behavioural alternatives for, the dynamics of

'high vs low' networks. For example: better negotiating strategies for 'high' and 'low', the development of a framework for regular negotiations between high and low.

4.4   HIGH vs MIDDLE vs LOW

Behavioural tendencies and central problems

Our focus in the network type 'high vs middle vs low' is on the middle position. The classic problem of the middle position is role conflict: high assigns a task, low acts at cross purposes and the man in the middle is caught in between! A great many studies of middle positions focus on this problem; for example the foremen and supervisors in factories.

Van de Vliert (1977) developed a model for this type of situation which gives seven behavioural alternatives for 'middle'. In his view, there are a fixed number of ways of reacting to this type of role conflict. In principle, a middle manager can make a very conscious and well-considered choice from the following:

1. He can shift the role conflict to the two parties with contrasting expectations of him, letting them fight it out together;
2. He can try to get one or both parties to change its expectations;
3. He can lead a double life by alternately agreeing with high or low, depending on whom he is dealing with;
4. He can try to satisfy both parties;
5. He can choose one of the parties;
6. He can avoid the role conflict by stalling and by keeping away from both parties;
7. He can evade the entire situation by reporting sick or by taking a different job.

Another frequent problem in middle positions is role ambiguity. For instance, it may be unclear what his boss really expects of him in the way of tasks and competence. Or he has no idea what role his subordinate attributes to him; perhaps, too, the subordinate has no clear expectations.

We can try to remedy role ambiguity and role conflict in several ways: a more precise job description, management by objectives, better communication with the superior. Organizational consultants have developed special interventions such as the role analysis technique, the job expectation technique and role negotiating (French and Bell, 1984; Huse, 1980).

But the question remains whether these strategies and interventions can ward off difficulties. In view of the persistence with which the same problems keep coming up in studies about the man in the middle, perhaps it is a structural problem, a problem that has to do with his characteristic position between the more and the less powerful. Are there not a few insoluble dilemmas here?

Roethlisberger (1944) stated it as follows:

The crux of the foreman's problem is that he is constantly faced with the dilemma of (1) having to keep his superior informed with what is happening at the work level and (2) needing to communicate this information in such a way that it does not bring unfavourable criticism on himself for not doing his job correctly or adequately. Discrepancies between the way things are at the work level and the way they are represented to be by management cannot be overlooked, and yet the foreman feels obliged to overlook them when talking to his boss. This makes the foreman's job particularly 'tough' and encourages him to talk out of both sides of his mouth at the same time—to become a master of double talk.

Dutch research of middle management mentioned role ambiguity and irritated relations with the superior and with the subordinates as the most important causes of stress (COP, 1979, p. 50). According to the researchers, irritable relations with the boss were largely due to his putting more emphasis on mistakes than on what was done properly. This is in line with Roethlisberger's statement above. This study of middle-management jobs repeatedly mentioned the buffer function as a typical characteristic.

The tensions and the pressure that are felt are ascribed to the specific nature of the job, in which one is responsible for daily problems and at the same time occupies a buffer position between management and task performers (COP, 1979, p. 27).

The most important tasks of middle management—serving the production interests of the firm and being responsible for the people in their department—are also the greatest sources of tension for them (COP, 1979, p. 29).

Middle management is sandwiched between two interest groups. Above them emphasis is on production; there concern interests are represented. Below them emphasis is on the interests of the workers (COP, 1979, p. 75).

Roethlisberger (1944, p. 290) also portrayed this problem markedly:

The foreman must (1) *uphold* at the work level the standards, policies, rules and regulations which have been originated by other groups and see to it that the workers *conform* to them, at the same time, (2) obtain if possible the workers' spontaneous *co-operation* to this way of doing business. . . . This is not a popular way of evoking spontaneity of co-operation. . . . Again and again, he is put in a position either of getting the workers' co-operation and being 'disloyal' to management or of being 'loyal' to management and incurring the resentment and overt opposition of his subordinates.

It looks like the ways of *solving* the built-in tensions are but limited for this type of position. The best thing you can do in such a job is compromise; perhaps you even need to be something of an opportunist!

Interventions

Roethlisberger (1944) concluded his article with several recommendations: increase mutual understanding, develop democratic leadership, be aware of people's personal needs, utilize insights to counter resistance to change, give consideration to the importance of the informal organization. This is quite vague. All of them are variants of the idea: more 'human' personal relations, good and open communication will bring about improvement!

The Dutch study of middle management and stress gave the following advice to teach middle management to utilize its buffer position:

- It is important to keep the quality of the *communication between* middle management and their superiors and subordinates good, i.e. do not be vague, but give and obtain sufficient information. This is generally only possible if the quality of the communication at the top of the company is good as well.
- Middle managers must be aware of their position and know what *expectations* people have of them. Management by objectives creates clarity in this respect.
- Middle management must *talk more concretely about the work* and *learn to* discuss *problems and possible solutions* better.
- Middle management must *not avoid differences of opinion or conflicts*, but accept them as facts of life or even as desirable, and talk them over.
- The interests, wishes and goals of the people 'above' and 'below' middle management are not by definition opposed. If they are clear on both sides, pressure on the buffer position will decrease. The buffer function can change into a co-ordinating function (COP, 1979, p. 76).

They saw three ways of arriving at greater clarity in the work situation:

1. Management by objectives;
2. Career counselling and guidance;
3. Support from the direct superior (COP, 1979, pp. 69ff).

Such recommendations somewhat overlook the dilemmas of middle management, dilemmas to which the researchers were certainly not blind. Does a person in such a position really stand to gain by greater clarity about his job? For the study also showed that a detailed job description and more and better regulations easily led to more stress and less satisfaction. 'A high degree of independence is not only necessary for good job performance, but is also a very important source of satisfaction in the work. However, autonomy is also one of the sources of ambiguity' (COP, 1979, p. 68).

Autonomy is not only effective and the source of satisfaction, it is *also* inhibiting and the source of stress. In truth, this is not an easy problem to solve! And it is doubtful whether improved communication, in the sense of 'talking more concretely about the work' and 'not avoiding differences of opinion or conflicts but talking them over', offers much solace. Perhaps these are very healthy strategies of self-protection. For according to the research, the man's superior criticizes him as soon as something goes wrong somewhere and superiors have a great tendency to emphasize mistakes. Furthermore, superiors are sometimes prone to intervene directly, over the heads of middle management.

Keeping things vague, covering up conflicts or making light of them are not only important ways for the middle manager to stay on his feet himself. They also help him to keep separate two parties for which bringing matters into the open and perhaps even to a head would probably do more harm than good.

Finally, even assuming that the interests of 'high' and 'low' are not by definition opposed, it is doubtful whether the buffer function can be changed into a co-ordinating function. Not by definition opposed? In concrete situations they are all too often perceived this way. And first and foremost by the man it is all about, the one in between. 'Good communication' may perhaps help, but in view of the structural difficulties involved, we should not be very optimistic about its effects. We therefore need to turn our attention to two additional and entirely different types of recommendations.

These recommendations tackle the formal nature of the problems and propose *structural changes*. For instance, *horizontalization of the organization*, implying fewer middle positions, and giving the remaining levels more clearly defined powers and competence: *vertical task expansion*. One argument in favour of this is formed by indications that the power of middle positions has been serious eroded. At any rate, it is quite evident for the foreman's position. Miller (1967) relates this to five developments:

1. Foremen are beset by management and consultants with pleas not to act in an authoritarian manner. They are expected to be mindful of the social aspects of leadership, but may not get too close to their subordinates.
2. Foremen used to be nearly autonomous in technical matters of production. Now they have to leave everything to the technical department, to maintenance, etc.
3. Recruitment, selection, dismissal, transfer, bonuses, etc., were formerly tasks of a foreman. They have now been taken over by the personnel department.
4. A wide variety of relatively new departments such as production control, organization quality control, planning and finance have further deflated his task. In addition, he is often expected to report to them in detail and to make sure they do not bother his staff.
5. The rise of in-company organizational forms for promoting employees' interests (in the Netherlands, the works council and sometimes shop-floor organizations). This causes the pressure from below to increase and also provides an opportunity to go behind the foreman's back.

Conclusion: the position of foreman has lost a good deal of its power and has been given nothing but obligations in its place. No wonder the man in the middle has a hard time of it!

If we cannot or do not want to change the structure, then it is a good idea to consider re-evaluating the strategies people use in such a situation. This involves an acceptance of the social skills that are evidently effective and legitimate means of functioning: making concessions, cajoling and covering up. And to use Roethlisberger's terms, why not become 'a master of double talk'? Did not Ritzer (1972, p. 1976) say: 'Double talk is another creative form of role conflict resolution which can be included under the category of independent action'?

It is perhaps more effective to adopt an active power strategy of obligating your subordinates to you, conniving and granting them small favours. (According to research of role conflict situations, this occurs frequently and works well: Dalton, 1954, Ch. 13; Brusky, 1959, pp. 452–72; Roethlisberger and Dickson, 1939, pp. 450–1; Sykes, 1956, pp. 257–62; Ulrich *et al.*, 1950, p. 39; Walker *et al.*, 1956, pp. 71–2).

The prestige thus obtained makes possible accomplishments which will please the foreman's immediate superior—but only if it is offset by certain favours. Some findings show that a greater influence on 'high' offers a better chance of influencing 'low' (Likert, 1961, pp. 113–14). And the circle is closed. Veen (1979, p. 11) was referring to the same dynamic when he stated that the interests of superior–foreman–subordinates are seldom entirely parallel. 'A foreman will need to acquire the necessary elbow-room from his superior. This gives him influence with his subordinates, increasing his chances of success, which in turn gives him more leeway with respect to his superior, etc.'

Summary of high vs middle vs low

In summary, there are three approaches to the problems of middle positions (role conflict and role indistinctness, stress).

1. The organizational development approach, which sets out to improve human relations. We attempt to do so through more open communication, greater clarity about tasks and powers, talking over differences of opinion, etc.
2. The structural approach, which means to resolve recurrent problems by intervening in the power relations of the network. For instance, removing the middle position or providing it with a reasonable power base.
3. Acceptance of insights and skills which have traditionally been used to cope with such situations. Examples: compromise, cajole, obligate both high and low to you, find a strategy to develop your own power so that you are not trapped between high and low.

Depending on the situation, a *combination* of these tactics will probably work best. The approaches under (2) and (3) are not really considered often enough.

Higher in the pyramid

The closer we come to the top of an organization, the fewer studies we find about the problems of 'the man in the middle'. Here a different aspect starts to dominate. Mulder (1977) reasoned that the closer one is to the top of an organization, the more one is out to get still closer to the top. Competing for top positions may become rather demanding: a person is dependent on people whom he hopes to equal, or even to surpass. Zaleznik and Kets de Vries (1975) claimed that people who have the capacity to work together closely with a figure of authority without falling into infantile dependency relations have the best chances.

There is a second central problem at this level. One is competing with colleagues of the same level, colleagues on whom one is dependent to some extent and with whom one must maintain reasonable relations. Much more is needed to cope with these two problems than a defensive clinging to one's autonomy. An active, flexible and adept manner is required.

A few examples of the tactics of 'lieutenants' in such a situation: without openly pitting themselves against colleagues, they try to present themselves as stronger and better by showing more initiative, doing work of high quality. Especially important are tangible and conspicuous achievements, feats remarkable enough to attract attention.

Korda (1975) wrote captivatingly and extensively about the sort of behaviour and the attributes that can serve to support a power position. One of the things he mentioned was the importance of clear insight into the existing power relations, formal as well as informal, and the development of a relational network that provides access to more powerful persons and makes appropriate coalitions possible.

For interventions at this level, it is important to keep in mind the difficulty participants in such a network have to 'stay on their feet'. In this context, Zaleznik and Kets de Vries (1975) disparage sensitivity training as a dangerous form of ritualism. At any rate, in my view, forms of advice and counselling that demand a great deal of openness, mutual trust and intensive feedback of the participants are not easy to practise. This is not to say that no team development is possible at this level. Elucidating the ways in which people are dependent on one another and what they see as obstacles to effective functioning can be important starting-points. Other possible approaches are a strong task orientation, or learning to deal constructively with conflicting interests.

It is important that an interventionist takes the various interests on the table seriously. Openness and trust, the common interest and organizational goals do not always help us in such a situation. Sometimes these things fall into the category of rhetoric which is already overused in organizations to cover up the reality of 'political' bickering. It may be socially desirable for a consultant to take part in it, but it may also be a pitfall.

Table 4.6   Outline of how power relations function

Types of power relations	Behavioural tendencies and problems	Interventions
Equal vs equal O——O——O	*Suboptimization* • Tendency to compete with one another • Covert fighting for positions • Constant friction in border areas	• Defining demarcation lines • Improving co-ordination procedures • Integrating units • Teaching negotiating skills • Clarifying common interest • Activating central authority
High vs low (triangle: O over O—O)	*Control vs autonomy* • Resistance to change • The motivation problem	• Bureaucratizing power through rules • Different style of leadership • Clarifying the 'pitfalls' • Structural and cultural interventions (OD)
High vs middle vs low (O–O triangle with O at top)	*Role conflict, role ambiguity, stress* • Concessions, double talk, use of sanctions and rewards to strengthen the position	• Improving communication • Clarifying tasks • Horizontalization, vertical task expansion • Teaching 'power strategies'

4.5   SUMMARY

Table 4.6 gives an outline of the main types of power relations, behavioural tendencies and organizational problems, and possible interventions.

The intention of this chapter has been to make clear that much behaviour and many problems are inherent in certain organizational relations. *We often have to deal with inevitable contrasts and dilemmas that are built into power and dependency relations. It is not easy to resolve these problems. Regulating them, making sure tensions do not escalate, may be more realistic.*

We have given our vision of what part consultants can play in these relations. Of primary importance are improvements in the structure, such as an active power base in equal vs equal, closely knit organizational frameworks in high vs low and horizontalization or vertical task expansion in high vs middle vs low. In the second place, we should be aware that negotiating, compromising, 'political' manœuvring and stratègies for gaining power can be legitimate manners of dealing with some types of problems. We have tried to indicate in what situations consultants can expect this sort of behaviour and to make suggestions about how to deal with it. Gaining acceptance for negotiating and power strategies and having people utilize them more realistically and more effectively may turn out to be important interventions. We must be careful with easy recommendations of 'open communication', 'talk over problems well', 'frankness' and 'intensive feedback'.

This chapter has worked out one aspect of relations: power relations. Relations between subunits in organizations have several aspects. We discussed the nature of these interdependencies in Chapter 2. The next chapters will treat them more thoroughly. Three sorts of relations will be distinguished. Extensive intervention arsenals have been given for two of them. But the decision-making about the allocation of 'scarce resources' among interdependent subunits is still more or less virgin territory. Chapter 5 will be devoted to this.

4.6 CONSEQUENCES FOR CONSULTANCY: TWO EXAMPLES

We will briefly present two examples as illustrations of how the prototypes of power relations can be useful for understanding the problems and for searching for adequate interventions.

1. Equal vs equal: negotiate or power base

This case is about restructuring the health-care facilities in a certain region. The reason consultants were called in was the impending closure of a local hospital. The consultants were asked to study the health care in this region and to make concrete proposals for its improvement. After a very thorough and extensive study, the consultants worked out a concrete plan based on:

(a) premises that had been formulated together with several independent professors of medicine;
(b) government criteria and norms for health-care facilities;
(c) figures on expected developments;
(d) a participative procedure.

This could lead to a high-quality and creative solution for the health care in that region.

The matter came to an impasse which has lasted several years. Nothing is being done with the study. An *analysis of the network* showed there were seven interest groups, including doctors, health insurance funds, government (national, provincial, local) and hospital boards. There is no central authority which stands above the parties. The lines of communication between the groups are underdeveloped. There is no co-ordinating body with representatives of the parties, but there is organized consultation among the hospital boards involved.

The interest of the groups involved are far from clear. Several boards, some groups of personnel, doctors and specialists, and local population groups are fearful of their positions being jeopardized and their security undermined.

Commentary

The case was discussed with several consultants and the chief conclusions were: (1) the creation of a central authority with regulatory powers should have had priority; (2) perhaps organizing and chairing structured and intensive negotiations among representatives of the most important groups would have increased the chances of reaching a solution; the matter was approached too much as a rational and technical problem.

A consultant with a great deal of experience in such projects told how he had repeatedly seen it happen that, if there was no power base, no central authority that could make decisions at a certain point, the matter nearly always became deadlocked. From then on, his first focus of attention was the composition of the network. 'No power centre? And one can't be created? Don't accept it! Research and recommendations are senseless!'

Conclusion: here we have to do with a fairly complex 'equal vs equal' network with the usual characteristics: escalating tendencies (pressure groups indeed took to the streets), the risk of an impasse and unmanageability. To get around this, the creation or activation of a co-ordinating central authority is required; if necessary, a structured negotiating process can be set up for those directly involved. The network was not developed in this direction; however, a good plan was presented for the co-ordination of health-care activities. The impasse continues.

2. A fluctuating power balance: loss and restoration of position

This case took place in a large company. It involved a research and development department. Relations, primarily with production but also with the management, were worsening. Research felt that production paid too little regard to research results. 'It is production that is remiss. They don't listen to us.' Production claimed that research was not pragmatic enough, that things took too long, that returns were too low, etc. Research, and more specifically the head of the department, acquired a bad name from all this bickering. The central management dictated, 'Reduce costs, be more pragmatic, even if it means lowering scientific sights', as important criteria. Internal differences of opinion and opposition arose. Relations with production grew more and more irritated. Characteristics of escalation to a confrontation situation, such as the avoidance of direct contact and the mobilization of 'constituencies', became more and more manifest. The position of the head of the research department became weaker both internally and externally.

In talks with the consultant it became apparent that research wanted to deal with the matter among themselves. They were not at all in favour of discussing matters with production, for instance. Together with the consultant, they decided to spend several days deliberating among themselves. Relations with production were naturally a very important topic of the talks. An important conclusion was that their manner was too 'bossy'; they did too much controlling and too little supporting. They put this conclusion into practice in a different attitude and different behaviour towards others.

A second topic that was given a lot of attention was internal relations and the style of leadership. It proved to be possible to talk over the contrasts that lay here and to arrive at workable agreements about the future. In retrospect, these two results turned out to 'work' well; contacts with the central management and production improved, there were fewer personal irritations and better co-ordination.

Commentary

The most important questions to be asked about this case are:

1. What was it that made research decide to do something about the matter? It is fairly normal to find some tensions between research and production. Why did they become acute?
2. Why did research not want a confrontation with production and central management about matters that concerned them jointly?

If we take a look at the network, we see several developments which were seriously impairing the position of research with respect to production and central management. The impaired position, be it the cause or the result of the concrete issues, made the matter acute and urgent. It was also the reason why research did not want to attempt a confrontation with other 'positions'. They were worried that their own position would come across as weak and not very defensible. It might lead to rigorous measures such as the dismissal of the head of the research department. This fear was concretely expressed: 'If we take this outside right now, the head of the department will be washed up.'

In short, they were expecting their own strategic position in the network to be further impaired. This weak position limited the possibilities for action. At the same time it was the incentive behind some drastic adjustments in their own circle: putting internal affairs in order, taking a different tack with respect to production. These two changes served to strengthen their position.

Summarizing: they realized they had been too ambitious in their relation to production. Once they saw the balance had tilted heavily against them, they brought things back in equilibrium by improving their internal organization and by putting a stop to the struggle for competence and replacing it with direct support, which gave them another chance to prove themselves. Their position was safeguarded.

I think that we cannot really account for the course of events here without looking at the nature of the network and the changes in the power relations. This is another 'equal vs equal' network in which the importance of maintaining and strengthening one's position in the strategic web stands out.

Here we clearly see a fluctuating power balance. It was impossible for them to improve their position. On the contrary: they ended up in a high vs low relationship. From there, they managed to tip the scales more in their favour. *An astute piece of work, because in such a situation it is easy for 'low' to pout and adopt a sullen attitude.* They sensed very well that such an attitude is not a good basis for discussion and solution.

5 Negotiating Relations

5.1 INTRODUCTION

A great many studies have been devoted to task-oriented and socio-emotional skills. Power behaviour and negotiating in organizations, on the other hand, have received much less attention. This book was written in response to that need. Power has been extensively discussed. Negotiating is the subject of this chapter.

Until recently, negotiating as a specific skill to cope with problems in organizations has been sorely neglected. Consultants frequently introduce and develop highly task-oriented social skills such as meeting techniques, decison-making and problem-solving. They also encourage the use of socio-emotional skills: a wide range of training and forms of team development make abundant use of interventions involving feedback, self-actualization, promoting frankness and understanding.

These are important and useful skills, but in situations of divergent interests and little mutual trust, they can only be of limited use. As an organizational consultant, I have taken part in a large number of discussions and meetings in a great many organizations. Although it never occurred to anyone to call these meetings negotiations, that was precisely what they were. Some of them were conducted so clumsily that extended impasses threatened or the situation escalated to open or more covert hostility, an unintentional and often needless development!

These experiences have made it clear to me how negotiating skills can play a constructive role. I have also seen how quickly people pick things up in this field. It is a type of behaviour which everyone deals with every day. Whether we want to or not, whether we realize it or not, we all negotiate. With this in mind, it never fails to amaze me how clumsily people sometimes go about it. Examples of behavioural tendencies are:

- confusing negotiating with scoring points;
- trying to find out who is right;
- neglecting the climate: 'let's get down to business';

- overlooking the fact that the relationship with the 'constituency' is a negotiating relation;
- thinking negotiations have failed when matters reach an impasse;
- confusing tenacious negotiating with obstinacy;
- being blind to the characteristics of one's negotiating style and its effects on others;
- not recognizing manipulations of oneself and others;
- seeing adjournments as a sign of weakness;
- viewing a joint search for solutions as giving in.

Many organizational problems have negotiating aspects. An organization is composed of interdependent units which have their own interests as well. Every important decision in organizations involves some degree of tug-of-war between interested parties. Policy formulation, cut-backs, the allocation of personnel, budgets, powers, important projects, space in buildings, secretarial support, automation facilities—all of these are issues in which negotiation plays a role.

Recent developments in organizations, which were treated in Chapter 3, further strengthen the need for constructive negotiation. I am referring to tendencies to decentralization, smaller, more autonomous units, a stronger market orientation, a more entrepreneurial climate. Organizational divisions are more and more thrown back upon their own responsibility. Less intervention by higher up goes hand in hand with stronger horizontal rivalry. This tendency towards greater autonomy and more responsibilities makes a stronger appeal to the capacity to negotiate with 'rival' interests inside and outside the organization in order to reach agreement.

I have gradually come to see negotiating as a skill that can successfully combine self-interests with interdependency. And more than that: negotiating can even increase the value of interdependency in the sense that people learn better how to take advantage of it.

The following Section 5.2 is the latest in a series of studies showing a gradual integration of insights into negotiating (Mastenbroek, 1977, 1979, 1980a,b, 1984). This integration came about as follows. Based on a study of the literature, four angles were chosen which seemed the most fruitful for a better understanding of negotiating. They were:

(a) Negotiating as a set of tactical rules of thumb. There are a great many of these dos and don'ts. It is interesting and useful material, but must be ordered and classified;
(b) Negotiating as a skill based on the handling of several dilemmas. Material on this is scattered throughout the literature. This is an angle I worked out in more detail.
(c) Negotiating as a process with a structure in time. The phases of this process can be found in the model described here.
(d) Negotiating as a complex of different types of activities. One classic study (Walton and McKersie, 1965) is based on this. The basic principle has

been incorporated, but a largely different typology of basic activities was developed.

The material was further developed over the years. Of primary concern was to make it more recognizable and applicable. Systematic interviews and group discussions with experienced negotiators shaped and modelled the original substance. In a wider sense, a great many conferences with very divergent types of negotiators also greatly contributed to it. Concepts which were difficult to recognize disappeared, as did insights which were considered impracticable. Profiting from the knowledge and the experience of skilled negotiators and their challenging questions and critical remarks, I made all kinds of alterations and additions. For example, from an original list with twelve negotiating dilemmas, only four remained, and all four of them were drastically reformulated.

One could hardly call this a logical process; it was more trial and error. Variants were developed and tried out, sometimes on the basis of experiences and observations, sometimes in discussions with interested persons, sometimes in conferences. A series of simulations of 'real' negotiation experiences and problems outlined more and more clearly the notions about the essential 'levers'. This gradually led to a lucid and workable model to be used as a backdrop in preventing problems and avoiding undesired destructive behaviour. This model is presented in the second part of this chapter. In the third part, a few theoretical and practical implications of the model will be discussed.

5.2   NEGOTIATING

Introduction

Organizations are differentiated further and further into functions and specialisms. Longer and longer chains of dependency come about. Familiar mechanisms such as control from above, intervention by a higher level on the hierarchical ladder or formal authority are often no longer present or feasible.

Situations in which power differences are no longer decisive and in which parties have different interests but are also dependent on one another are negotiating situations. What can we systematically say about negotiating? A model of negotiating will be described below which is based on two basic dimensions of social behaviour:

(a) the co-operation–fighting dimension;
(b) the exploring–avoiding dimension.

These two dimensions have *their foundations in a conditioning factor interdependency*. The inevitable choices on both dimensions are influenced by the nature of the interdependency, or rather by the balance of power between the parties. Together these two dimensions show the possible ways of coping with various forms of interdependency.

Research and theory formation

Negotiating has recently become a subject of important consideration for social science. Rubin and Brown (1975) summarized several hundreds of studies. But here we encounter the problem of too many studies with too many different outcomes. It is not an easy matter to integrate them.

Negotiating: when is it appropriate?

First of all, we can see negotiating as a particular social skill to be distinguished from other social skills such as 'co-operation' and 'fighting'.

- *Co-operation* is appropriate when one has similar interests and goals. It is the obvious solution if the benefits for those involved depend directly on the extent to which they can pool their resources.
- *Negotiating* is the proper strategy if there are different, sometimes even contrasting interests, but if at the same time the two parties are interdependent in a way that an agreement would yield advantages for both of them. The parties disagree, but they would like to arrive at an agreement because letting things drift or fighting are disadvantageous for both of them.
- *Fighting* is the most likely strategy when, in the case of opposed interests, one party thinks he stands to gain more by fighting than by negotiating. Sometimes it is adopted as a strategy for turning a position of powerlessness into a firm negotiating position with respect to another party. A fighting strategy is concerned with obtaining dominance and reducing the opponent to submission.

The boundaries between these three approaches are not clear-cut. We might readily think of them as a continuum. As we have seen (p. 53), the degree of interdependence is the best criterion in the choice of the proper strategic behaviour on this continuum. Table 5.1 serves to illustrate the three strategies.

In negotiating situations, we are sometimes faced by difficult decisions because they are permeated by our own interests *and* by mutual dependency. Too often people are blind to anything but their own manifest interests. This makes them opt for a harder strategy than is in accordance with the strong interdependency. If they later discover that they have not foreseen the unfavourable consequences, there is often *so* much mutual mistrust that co-operation is almost impossible. On the other hand, people sometimes too quickly opt for a co-operative strategy in situations which demand quite some caution about their own position. If attempts to co-operate do not have the expected effects, they feel disappointed and manipulated. Then there is a strong tendency to turn to fighting behaviour or to yield.

Generally, it is remarkable how easily people allow themselves to be drawn into fighting behaviour. It is often motivated by referring to the less construc-

Table 5.1   Tactics used in co-operation, negotiation and fighting

Co-operation	Negotiation	Fighting
Conflict is seen as a common problem	Conflict is seen as a clash between different but mutually dependent interests	Conflict is seen as a question of 'winning or losing', 'over or under', 'we or they'
People present their own goals as accurately as possible	People exaggerate their own interests but pay attention to possible areas of agreement	People emphasize the superiority of their own objectives
Weak points and personal problems can be openly discussed	Personal problems are disguised or presented very circumspectly	Personal problems are treated as if they do not exist
The information provided is honest	The information given is not false, but one-sided. The facts favourable to one's own party are deliberately emphasized	If it can help to make the opponent submit, false information is deliberately spread
Discussion subjects are presented in terms of underlying problems	Agenda items are formulated in terms of alternative solutions	Points of disagreement are formulated in terms of one's own solution
Possible solutions are tested against their practical consequences	Occasionally the linking of solutions to principles is used to put some pressure on the other side	One's own solutions are rigidly tied to higher principles
Commitment to one particular solution is deliberately delayed as long as possible	Strong preference for a particular solution is shown, but margins and concessions are taken for granted	An absolute and unconditional preference for one's own solution is expressed at every opportunity
Threats, confusion and taking advantage of the mistakes of others are seen as detrimental	Occasionally a modest and carefully calculated use is made of threats, confusion and surprise	Threats, confusion, shock effects, etc., are welcome at any time to reduce the opponent to submission
Active participation of all concerned is encouraged	Contacts between parties are limited to only a few spokespersons	Contacts between the parties take place indirectly via 'declarations'
An attempt is made to spread power as much as possible and to let it play no further role	Power is occasionally tested, or attempts are made to influence the balance of power in one's own favour	Both parties engage in a permanent power struggle by strengthening their own organizations, increasing independence and dividing and isolating the opponent
People try to understand one another and share one another's personal concerns	Understanding the views of the other side is seen as a tactical instrument	No one bothers to understand the opponent
Personal irritations are expressed to clear the air of tensions that could hamper future co-operation	Personal irritations are suppressed or ventilated indirectly (e.g. with humour)	Irritations confirm negative and hostile images. Hostility is expressed to break down the other side
Both parties find it easy to call in outside expertise as an aid to decision-making	Third parties are brought in only if there is a complete deadlock	Outsiders are welcome only if they are 'blind' supporters

tive behaviour of the opponent. But the opponent sees it exactly the same way. And so the vicious circle goes on.

Research into negotiating (Rubin and Brown, 1975, pp. 130–6) has again and again pointed out these sorts of processes in which the parties manœuvre so clumsily that they become constricted in conflicts and struggles for prestige, thus seriously weakening both of them. Such processes are often spontaneous and, in a certain sense, unintentional. At some point, parties will realize that they are caught up in a spiral of growing hostilities. Insight into these *'spontaneous' dynamics* and a large arsenal of behavioural alternatives can help prevent unwanted behavioural tendencies towards destructive conflicts. Negotiating skills have too long been neglected in this arsenal. To be able to take advantage of negotiating, it is important to see it as a type of activity which is appropriate to certain sorts of dependency relations. Negotiation is a balancing act between different poles.

This concept of negotiation as several dilemmas deduced from the central polarity between co-operation and fighting will be combined below with a perspective of negotiating as four activities to produce a co-ordinating model.

Negotiating: four activities

Negotiating involves a mixture of four activities:

1. Obtaining substantial results;
2. Influencing the balance of power;
3. Promoting a constructive climate;
4. Obtaining procedural flexibility.

We will discuss each of these four activities. The section 'Negotiating effectively: conclusions' summarizes this negotiating model.

1. Obtaining substantial results

Generally, aspects of negotiating aimed at tangible results receive the most attention. I am referring to activities which focus on the *contents* of the negotiations such as: arguments, facts, standpoints, goals, interests, basic assumptions, compromise proposals, concessions and conditions. Negotiators try to influence the distribution of costs and benefits in a way favourable to them in matters of content. For example:

- by creating 'change';
- by disguising their proposals as ultimatums;
- by presenting favourable facts;
- by making only small concessions.

The most important activities are:

- a tactical exchange of *information* about goals, expectations and acceptable solutions;

Table 5.2   The dilemma of 'conceding vs stubborn'

1	2	3	4	5

Lenient, indulgent	Tenacious, testing	Hard, stubborn
Information and arguments are presented as open for discussion	Firm presentation of facts and arguments, but margins are taken for granted	Information and arguments are presented as self-evident and unassailable
The interests of the other side are accepted as they are	The interests of the other party are tested in order to discover its priorities	The interests of the opponent are challenged or belittled
Generous concessions facilitate the working out of compromises	Concessions are part of the game, but impasses are allowed to occur	Tendency to set ultimatums in order to provoke crises

- presenting one's *position* in a way that influences the perception of the other of what is attainable.
- working step by step towards a compromise with *concessions* on both sides.

The tactical choices a negotiator must make here can be understood as balancing between yielding and more persistent or even obstinate behaviour. Table 5.2 will illustrate this dilemma. Several tactics are commonly used to cope with this dilemma. They will be discussed here under the categories tactical use of information and choice of position.

Tactical use of information. The tactical exchange of information has two purposes:

(a) to find the opponent's bottom offer and to bring it down further;
(b) to clarify one's own demands in such a way that the opponent will see them as realistic and inevitable.

In a nutshell: *influencing the 'attainabilities'*.
Tactical information can be provided in several ways. They include:

- information in which a concession is inflated in the hope that one will thus not have to make any further concessions;
- choosing examples selectively.

Closely related to the way in which one provides or obtains information is the manner in which one chooses a position at the start of the negotiations.

Choosing a position. We must distinguish between the tactic of the definitive choice and that of the open choice. The tactic of the *definitive choice* has several variants:

- 'take it or leave it';
- the ultimatum;

- accomplished facts;
- 'final offer first'.

The last one is the toughest variant. It implies that one of the parties presents his proposals as final and as really the last word straight away at the outset of the negotiations. Such a tactic has a few very clear advantages. One takes the initiative and forces the other on the defensive. One places responsibility for a possible breakdown in the negotiations with the other party. Furthermore, immediately choosing a position creates a reputation of resolute seriousness and credibility. This can be very important for future negotiations. But it also involves considerable risk. It makes it very hard to go back without a serious loss of face, even if it later appears that some things have been overlooked. Particularly if the relationship is poor, the other party will feel it has no choice, and this in itself can arouse much resistance.

Often parties enter into negotiations with an *open choice of position*, sometimes in a sort of preliminary discussion. They may make statements about their own interests and about their own view of what is to be done. This gives a maximum of room to manœuvre. Sometimes one opens with an extreme position but occupies it flexibly. Generaly speaking, this is not very sensible because it can erode a person's credibility. Such a position choice is felt to be opportunistic. If a position really must be taken, it is generally best to start with 'the highest defensible claim'. This implies that a person can prove his claims and that he has created elbow-room.

2. Influencing the balance of power

The course negotiations take is related to the power and dependency relations. The interdependency may be unequally divided between the parties. But negotiating assumes *a certain equality* between parties. When there are clear power differences, different behaviour occurs. A certain balance of power and an awareness that both parties need each other are conditions for constructive negotiating.

And yet the parties do test each other's strengths and probe the precise division of dependency. The *dilemma* here is that a stronger position can provide an advantage at the negotiating table, but that an opponent does not like to see his or her own power position weakened and will do everything possible to prevent it. If this happens, not much will come of negotiating. It becomes a power struggle; it shifts in the direction of fighting behaviour. So a careful strategy is required. But again not too careful, because an opponent may regard too little defensibility as a way to obtain the advantage; it invites him to exploit the situation, as it were. This dilemma is summarized and clarified with examples of tactics on the power axis in Table 5.3.

There are different *ways of strengthening one's own power position at the negotiating table*. Below they are summed up and their effects discussed.

'Fighting'. These are tactics which are directly aimed at subjugating the opponents. Examples are:

Table 5.3   The dilemma 'bending vs domineering'

1	2	3	4	5

Minimal resistance	Preserving a certain balance	Aggressive, trying to dominate
Restrained use of 'favourable facts', pressure is avoided	Attempting to influence the balance by means of facts and careful dosage of pressure	Influencing the balance by means of threats, manipulation, confusion and arrogance
Little resistance when challenged	When challenged, one reacts in proportion to the situation	When challenged, one attacks
No active interest in alternatives to the current relationship	Alert to alternatives for improving one's position *within the current relationship*	Pretending to have a great many alternatives; acting as though one will break off the relationship at the least sign of trouble

- behaving obstinately;
- ignoring the other party's information and arguments;
- feigning emotions such as anger and impatience;
- not listening, or only listening to 'weak points';
- stating an absolute preference for one's own solution;
- leaving the other party no choice;
- sowing dissension.

When such means are employed, it generally means escalation. The other party will soon start to fight back. It is best to use them in small doses if they are to be used at all. They should be not so much a manner of achieving authority, but more a means of obtaining information about how staunchly the other side upholds its view. Perhaps one will use them to show a little healthy resistance to fighting behaviour by the other side. The idea is to keep this pressure temporary and not gradually *to set in motion a process of growing hostility on both sides. A short, direct and hard confrontation is preferable to a series of skirmishes.*

Manipulating. This is a more indirect attempt to strengthen one's position at the negotiating table. The most subtle are the manipulations that effect a person's feeling of self-esteem; for instance, insisting on having one's way as if it was the only logical thing to do, or creating a hail-fellow-well-met atmosphere and then offhandedly shoving a proposal through the meeting. If one does not recognize the manipulation, it is difficult to counter. It gives a person the feeling he is an obstructionist who does not want to understand or who is spoiling the atmosphere. Although manipulation involves a lower risk of direct escalation, the effect can be the same in the long run. Even if the opponent does not recognize the fact that he is being manipulated, he intuitively feels resistance. Increasing tension and irritation at one's own powerless position will put the relationship under pressure. It is quite questionable whether this is in the interests of the manipulator!

Facts and expertise. Knowledge of the history, background information about the negotiating partners, having facts and material at hand which are favourable for one's own position and being able to present them with a certain show of expertise; these are all things that strengthen a person's position at the negotiating table. It is important that any facts presented are manifest and credible for the opponents as well. The way in which they are presented is also important. A triumphant manner, for instance, can create much ill-feeling: it combines the facts with a fighting attitude. Presenting them with a great show of self-evidence means linking them to a more manipulative approach.

Facts that carry a lot of weight in the balance of power between parties are the *alternatives* one has if no agreement is reached. The more alternatives, and the more attractive they are, the stronger is one's position.

Exploring. This technique, which we will treat at length (p. 93), can strengthen a person's position for different reasons. Exploring means a certain power of initiative: posing questions, giving information, making proposals, creating a possible package deal; by taking more such initiatives than the opponent, a verson increases his own strategic elbow-room. Exploring also means trying to consider the interests of the opponent; a person's attitude is characterized by 'How do *we* find a solution to this *together*?' This legitimates a person's performance, it lends a person authority.

Strengthening the relation. The relationship with the opponent can be strengthened by developing acceptance and trust (described on p. 92). Other ways are developing a stronger common interest and increasing the number of shared objectives. This means finding and implementing outcomes interesting to both parties on a larger number of topics. These techniques strengthen the *mutual* dependency. This means one cannot strengthen one's position unilaterally. At best we may state that, for a less powerful position, a strong increase in mutual dependency makes the relationship somewhat more symmetrical.

Power of persuasion. Elements of persuasive power are:

- A clear, well-structured manner of explaining one's own opinion;
- Reasonably relaxed attitude but not nonchalant;
- Variation: voice level, tempo, concrete examples *and* the general lines; use of visual aids;
- An emotional, slightly 'high-flown' commitment to one's own view, as long as it does not become rhetoric.

Manipulating and fighting can provide a temporary advantage but comprise the risk of escalation and irritated personal relations. The other ways are more constructive.

Strengthening the starting position. Once at the negotiating table, opportunities to influence the balance of power are but scarce. A person must have consolidated his position by this time. Important sources of power here are:

1. *Specialized knowledge* in certain fields. Preferably knowledge that is scarce and of vital importance.
2. Having a *broad background*. Having done your homework, having a bird's-eye view of the situation, knowledge of the history, knowledge of policy changes, having available all important documents.
3. Having *alternatives*. Not only alternative solutions for the items on the agenda, but also different ways of reaching your own goals, perhaps with others.
4. *'Political' access* and political intuition. Easy access to relevant centres of power is of special importance.
5. *Status*. Tangible success, informal authority, hierarchical position, personal trustworthiness, credibility—these are all matters that contribute to it.
6. *Support of others*. Having allies during the meeting, being able to obtain help and support from other groups not present. Not operating in isolation.

These are *'facts'* that will show their effectiveness at the negotiating table.

All activities between parties are coloured and modelled by the balance of power. No wonder negotiators are very sensitive to changes in the power and dependency balances. Sometimes they involve open challenges, but more often covert nudges or tugs at the balance of power. Both becoming less powerful and becoming more powerful bring about strong emotional impulses. It can be important to develop one's 'radar' in this field.

All activities at the negotiating table are *embedded* in the nature of the mutual dependency—how strong, how one-sided, how permanent it is. Negotiations will only take place if there is a certain amount of interdependency. If the interdependency is very lopsided, we see entirely different behavioural tendencies: 'requesting', ordering and exploiting vs more submissive and passive or aggressive, as described in Chapter 4.

3. *Promoting a constructive climate*

In general, one may state that the more negotiators use co-operative behaviour (information on the table, great willingness in concessions, no use of pressure), the easier it becomes to achieve a good relationship. However, it must be emphasized that this is not the art of negotiating. On the contrary, the challenge lies somewhere entirely different: *if parties consistently and persis-*

Table 5.4   The dilemma 'jovial vs hostile'

1	2	3	4	5

Jovial, confidential	Credible, solid	Hostile, irritated
Reliance on personal charm, tendency to tell lots of jokes, likes to become very close	Promotion of informal discussions, shows an interest in personal matters, moderate use of humour, consistent behaviour	Keeping opponent at arm's length, formal behaviour, sometimes sarcastic, shows irritation, seems unpredictable
Dependent: 'Your interest is my interest.'	Interdependent: 'What solution will *we* find?'	Independent: 'What can *I* get out of this?'

tently come up for their own interests, what are the chances of a good relationship?

The *dilemma* here is that a fighting atmosphere must be avoided. Trust and credibility are important. But at the same time, building up too personal a relationship or investing too much in trust and climate does not work either. It is readily seen as overbearing, or as weak and silly. Table 5.4 summarizes this.

We can classify the tactics to cope with this dilemma into three categories:

1. Separating the person of the negotiator from his behaviour that is causing tensions;
2. Avoiding behaviour which causes unnecessary tensions;
3. Utilizing opportunities for behaviour to reduce tension.

Separating person and behaviour. In the first place a clear awareness is needed of everyone's tendency to play the man rather than the ball, particularly when a person shows firm resistance. The temptation to eliminate tension in this way is great. A way out is to regard a hard attitude of the opponent as typical role behaviour which a person in that position or wearing that cap inevitably must exhibit. Put more simply: '*Keep playing the ball and not the man.*'

Avoiding unnecessary tension. A good example of generating unnecessary irritation is emphasizing the term 'reasonable' in talking about one's own party or proposals. Such messages, that we are *reasonable, constructive, open, frank, generous, positive*, etc., have little power of persuasion, but they do carry the implicit connotation that the opponent might very well be unreasonable and unconstructive. *Threats* can also yield much unnecessary irritation and resistance. It is better to mention the consequences as factually as possible: '*Don't threaten with thunder and lightning but just predict the weather.*'

A point which negotiators should keep in mind in this connection is causing a loss of face. Catching the opponent off guard, pulling a fast one, letting it be known quite subtly that you know exactly what the other party is after, making the most of the opponent's 'mistakes' are all examples of behaviour than can easily damage the negotiating climate.

Reduction of tension. Cautious formulation is not the only way to lower tension. In every negotiating situation there are certain opportunities which, if utilized, can contribute to a positive atmosphere. Examples:

- if any appreciation of the other party is possible, show it;
- show respect for a person's reasoning, even if you do not agree with it;
- show a sense of humour, be able to put your own hehaviour into perspective;
- chat informally about more personal matters or about current news.

Very important in this connection *are the minutes just before the negotiations*. Particularly if they expect a meeting to be difficult, everyone comes in tense. Two *tips*:

- seek informal contact, preferably at a somewhat more personal level. Examples: hobbies, holiday plans, previous common experiences;
- keep moving, try to greet several of those present and to have a chat with them.

4. Obtaining procedural flexibility

Here we want to go more systematically into *procedures* which facilitate the exploration of negotiating elbow-room. However hard and unyielding a position may be, it can still often be combined with great *procedural flexibility* in seeking favourable compromises. There is more than one way out of the wood! We must distinguish the *means* from the *goals*. Some negotiators are well able to combine flexibility of means with sticking to their own goals.

A fundamental dimension of negotiating behaviour is involved. We are talking about the extent to which a negotiator explores. Successful negotiators keep seeking very tenaciously for alternatives that are relatively satisfactory for both parties, without having to moderate their demands. This is greatly facilitated by an extensive exchange of information, trying out possible solutions, making tentative proposals, thinking aloud, sounding out the other party. The *integrative potential* is thus fully utilized. Exploring is a search for overlapping interests: are there common premises, are relatively small concessions possible that mean a lot to the opponent and vice versa, can a combination of mutual advantages be created in a package deal? The two poles of this behaviour are shown in Table 5.5.

To understand this polarity, it is important to see that one can be passive in an *ostensibly active manner*. Examples would be using the same arguments but formulating them differently, clinging tenaciously to one's original premises, ignoring new information, defending a particular solution through thick and thin, or turning it into a matter of principle. Such behaviour may

Table 5.5   Procedural flexibility: exploring vs avoiding

1	2	3	4	5

Flexible, searching, active	Calm, patient	Staying on one track, passive
Taking advantage of opportunities, impulsive	Taking time to weigh and analyse possibilities	Reliance on fixed procedures
Coming up with new ideas, ability to improvise	Trying to keep things consistent	Sticking to original stand, supplying more evidence that it is 'correct'
Creating alternatives	Open to alternatives	Repetitive, rigid

sometimes be tactically warranted, as long as one is aware that it is an entrenchment and thus puts a stop to the search for integrative potential, at least temporarily. Even though it looks very active and may be surrounded by great flurry, it is in fact only 'more of the same'. It means avoiding the search for a compromise and can very much start to resemble fighting behaviour. We also encounter a more innocent variant in which one calmly, almost banteringly, relates one's own standpoint and more or less leaves it at that, thus avoiding confrontations.

When to explore? Although it is no simple matter, exploring can very well be combined with tough negotiating. It must be emphasized that exploring has nothing to do with being 'soft', amicable or yielding. What it is about is well expressed in the following rule of thumb: 'Be firm but flexible!'

Next we will discuss the *different phases of negotiating*. We shall see that classifying negotiations into phases gives us something to go on in seeking effective procedures. The most important procedures will be worked out in the second part of this section.

Phases in negotiating

Negotiations go through different *phases*. Depending on the phase, there are different opportunities to exploration. We will distinguish four phases: (1) preparation; (2) initial choice of position; (3) search phase; (4) impasse and finalization.

1. The preparatory phase

Experienced negotiators always emphasize the importance of this phase, in which one must not only determine one's standpoint, but also one's strategy. A thorough preparation generally means a tendency for one's standpoint to harden, thus lowering the chances of an agreement. This can be overcome by exploring in two ways: (1) informal consultation; (2) setting down alternatives.

In informal consultation, the parties work towards an exchange of ideas on standpoints, common interests and background situations. They probe reactions, sound out what might be attainable. Decisions are not made. The parties avoid taking inviolable positions. No report is made. The parties are feeling out how much room there is to manœuvre, while their priorities are taking shape. Informal consultation might take place in a joint study group, an agenda committee or preliminary meetings.

If we can manage to concentrate on alternatives during the preparatory phase, we prevent people from sitting down at the negotiating table with more or less immutable positions. Brainstorming may be very helpful at this point: not invested in the best standpoint, but in what might be interesting options. The more alternatives the better.

2. Initial choice of position

At a certain moment there is a tendency to take a position and to present it adamantly as entirely logical. This often takes the form of assertive statements. One presents one's proposals, well supported by facts and arguments, as fair and reasonable. There is sometimes a tendency to open or covert criticism of others. This phase serves two purposes: (1) one defines the playing field and tries to reserve as much space as possible for oneself; (2) one proves to the constituency that one has their interests at heart. The exploratory side of this phase could consist of being attentive to signals from the various parties about where the primary issues and interests lie.

The more a person concentrates his initial choice of position on his view of the situation—the interests behind it, bottlenecks he wants to eliminate, objectives, assumptions—and the less on his concrete standpoint in the form of specific demands, the better this works. The former creates leeway and there are more opportunities to see points in common. In the latter case, the situation of claim against claim, position vs position, proposal and counterproposal will more readily arise. It more quickly turns into barter without looking into the chances of integration. Exploring here means asking questions to investigate and define the interests and the assumptions behind them.

3. Search phase

This leads to discussions in which both sides try to find out how staunchly the other side will defend its demands. One continues to present one's position as a logical answer which is in the common interest. Broadly speaking, there are two ways of exploring in this phase. The forms, however, are almost diametrically opposed.

1. Exploring by means of 'pressure'. Bluffing, threatening, increasing time pressure, refuting arguments of the other party, brandishing the common

interest are examples of tactics. It may look hard and fierce. There is a risk of escalation. And yet a great deal of information can be gathered during this phase. Reactions from the other side give indications of what is attainable. And the other side is entitled to know your priorities. So a little extra pressure about them can be a warranted means of providing information.

2. Exploring by means of a 'non-binding search'. Asking questions, trying out ideas, thinking aloud, once again going over the consequences of a particular idea, working out a point 'for fun', formulating a tentative proposal, formulating 'unripe' ideas for a solution, brainstorming: these are all ways of probing the integrative leeway.

Sometimes the two ways are alternated. Like this, the parties test each other while sounding out the possibilities for combinations of wants and interests. The negotiations can sometimes even take on the nature of a joint search in which all kinds of ideas and alternatives are actively combined and probed, preferably with no obligation. Purposely created misunderstandings throw matters into confusion. On the face of it, everything is still shrouded in mist. Nothing important is finished, everything still seems open. Yet gradually the contours of a possible agreement become clear.

So much happens during this phase that we can sometimes speak of three subphases: first, vigorous and detailed deliberations in which both sides may use strong pressure, then a maturation phase, followed by a phase of co-operative seeking. These subphases may repeat themselves (Himmelman, 1971).

4. Impasse and finalization

Various proposals are on the table. Time starts to press. The question is deadlocked. It becomes clear to all that matters have reached an impasse.

It may be very hard for inexperienced negotiators to restrain themselves from fighting behaviour at this point. More experienced negotiators have less difficulty with it. They often recognize this phase as part of the game.

Impasses have two exploratory possibilities: (1) they provide information about how rigorous the standpoints are; (2) they can give an impetus to creativity. Impasses are a sort of test of how tenacious parties are; they force people to look for leeway once more. At the same time they impel people towards a search for new, more creative solutions. Sometimes a package deal can offer a way out. In other cases the negotiations continue, taking a certain proposal as a 'platform'. The 'platform proposal' is amended until it has become acceptable. This demands a business-like attitude. One cannot give in to the tendency to hardening and escalation but must continue to search.

These phases can gel into unwritten but very strict rules: negotiating becomes a sort of ritual. A ritualized form of negotiating tends to reduce tensions and uncertainties. Its course becomes fairly predictable. It greatly increases opportunities to control and regulate conflicts. A disadvantage is that such a process may take a good deal of time.

Procedures in exploring

We will briefly elaborate some of the chief procedures used in exploring.

Always begin the negotiations with an exploratory phase. Particularly when there are already proposals on the table, this is easier said than done. There is a strong tendency to react to one another's proposals. *Do not confuse argumentation with exploration!* In debating, one defends one's own proposals and tries to weaken those of the other party. In the long run, so much energy is invested in one's own detailed standpoints that the negotiating leeway becomes almost nil. One cannot even consider anything else without a serious loss of face.

Try to find common criteria. Do the basic assumptions show any common ground? Are there norms and values that appeal to both parties? Are there policy statements which commit the parties?

There is a risk inherent in this: parties sometimes hope to gain concrete advantages by elevating certain statements to principles. If people are not careful, the result may be very lengthy negotiations about high-flown ideals. For parties will refuse to endorse criteria and principles unfavourable to them unless they are formulated so complexly or abstractly that they can be interpreted to their advantage in the 'real' negotiations. This is a serious risk, as parties are often superbly capable of linking their wants to higher principles. If no clear, workable criteria can be found, there are three other tangible options:

1. Focusing on common interests;
2. Having parties present alternatives;
3. Working with a 'platform proposal'.

Try to find common interests. Parties are interdependent, they need each other. What binds them is the overlap in interests. What will benefit both parties? Is there anything common to their interests? Be clear about your interests. Concrete details, specific information, consequences, etc., bring your interests to life; they help legitimate them, in the eyes of your opponent as well. Even if you do not agree with them, try to view the interests of the other side at least as a *part of the problem*.

Try to get as many alternatives on the table as possible. Do not commit yourself to a solution in the preparatory phase. Discuss in what direction a solution should be sought. Discuss possible solutions. Create elbow-room. Try to have formal or informal 'preliminary deliberations'. Probe each other's ideas and avoid choosing a pronounced position. At most, try to line up a few alternative solutions without anyone having to commit himself.

Work with a 'platform proposal'. A procedural step which can work very well is making a proposal and then amending it with other parties. Instead of defending one's own proposal through thick and thin, one simply asks under what conditions it would be acceptable to the other, what alterations the other party would like. It also gives you an opportunity to make suggestions of your own. A proposal can be amended in this way until an acceptable compromise has been reached. It can work very well, especially if the issues are complex. A broad proposal is made. The outline is filled out and elaborated in several rounds of talks.

This makes it theoretically possible to reduce the number of phases of negotiations to two: the *start-up* phase, in which parties exchange information on the basis of which a tentative and broad but non-binding agreement is formulated. It is merely an outline, a platform which will be used in the second phase as a basis for the negotiations about the concrete *substance*.

Exploring in impasses. If an impasse continues, a new proposal may be a good tactic. Alternatives developed at an earlier stage can prove their usefulness here. A good technique is sometimes to *incorporate the least objectionable elements* of the last proposal of the opponents in one's own proposal.

Impasses can freeze personal relations as well as standpoints. To keep matters *moving*, there are the following tactics. Note that none of these tactics is a true concession. They involve behaviour that promotes *change* rather than behaviour with a *cooling and rigidifying* effect.

- Look for more and different information instead of correcting information and assessing it negatively;
- Look for the problems that lie at the root of the impasse instead of convincing and threatening;
- Be more spontaneous rather than more formal; more creative rather than more repetitive;
- Emphasize equality and mutual dependency (for instance, by exploring the negative consequences of a lasting impasse) rather than acting superior or retreating;
- Show disillusionment instead of acting as if it does not matter;
- Adjourn and seek informal contact rather than sitting out the meeting.

If you find that your attempts to explore get no response and if you want to apply some pressure, 'clinging to and cultivating an impasse' is sometimes a good tactic. Be approachable but undertake little. This is a dimension which is at right angles to the axis of 'co-operation–fighting'. The dilemmas here differ fundamentally from the previous three, all of which are part of the 'co-operation–fighting' dimension.

In this section we have discussed a very important dimension of negotiating behaviour: 'exploring–avoiding'. Exploring has proved to be a way of linking co-operation to competition, interdependency to interests. Very concisely, be firm and flexible. Starting from mutual but divergent interests, utilize the integrative space.

Effective negotiating: conclusions

In *summary*, we may say that skilful negotiating primarily involves a complex of four activities:

1. Obtaining substantial results;
2   Influencing the balance of power;
3. Promoting a constructive climate;
4. Obtaining procedural flexibility.

1. Obtaining substantial results

This involves a person's choice of position as it is expressed in standpoints, proposals, arguments and concessions. How does he arrive at a compromise which is as favourable as possible for him?

2. Influencing the balance of power

Attempts to tilt the balance of power are inevitable, and when they meet little resistance, it evokes exploitative behaviour. But wanting to dominate, scoring points and being obstinate lead more readily to fighting than to negotiation. Choices can be set out on the bending–domineering axis.

3. Promoting a constructive climate

How does a person cope with personal relations? These behaviours can be set out on the jovial–hostile axis. Hard negotiating must not be confused with hostile, irritated or sulky behaviour. Being jovial and overbearing does not work either.

4. Obtaining procedural flexibility

This is how a person increases leeway in negotiations. How does he create flexibility, how does he maintain other options, how does he find integrative possibilities? This is primarily a question of procedures.

The combination of procedural flexibility with tenacity of substance is the solution to *a classic negotiating problem: how to promote one's own interests without being obstinate. Or: how to look for solutions jointly without giving in.*

In the activities under (2) and (3), we have seen that it is best to aim at the middle. Combined with tenacity of substance, they hold the solution to a

Table 5.6   Two profiles of negotiating

Negotiating as four types of activities, each of them with a different *goal*	Dilemmas	Examples of tactics
1. Obtaining *substantial results* Goal: *favourable compromise*	Conceding vs stubborn 1 2 3 4 5 Lenient, Tenacious Hard, indulgent stubborn	Firm presentation of facts and arguments but margins are taken for granted. Impasses are allowed to occur and used as a test; relatively small concessions are part of the game. Step-by-step compromises are sought. Deadlines
2. Influencing the *balance of power* Goal: *equilibrium or slight domination*	Bending vs domineering 1 2 3 4 5 Minimal Preserving Aggressive, resistance a certain trying to balance dominate	Trying to adjust the balance of power by means of facts and restrained pressure. When challenged, one reacts in proportion. Alert to alternatives to improve one's position within the current relationship. Combining a recognition of manipulations with appropriate counter-actions. Keeping the initiative
3. Promoting a *constructive climate* Goal: *positive personal relations*	Jovial vs hostile 1 2 3 4 5 Confidential, credible, sarcastic, jovial solid formal, unpredictable	Promoting informal discussion, showing interest in personal matters, moderate use of humour, consistent behaviour. Interdependence: 'What solution will *we* find'. Distinguishing role behaviour from the person. Avoids loss of face
4. Obtaining *procedural flexibility* Goal: *flexibility*	Exploring vs avoiding 1 2 3 4 5 Flexible, Calm, Staying on searching, patient one track, active repetitive	Asking questions, making or eliciting proposals, searching for new information. Brain-storming about tentative solutions, open to alternatives. Searching for a creative package deal. Using draft proposals to amend and elaborate.
	Profile of effective negotiating Profile of naïve negotiating	

second classic negotiating problem: how to promote one's own interests without being aggressive or hostile.

   The solutions to both classic problems once again underscore the 'both–and' nature of the model described here. People can integrate seeming contrasts in their behaviour.

We are now in a position to give a profile of effective negotiating. Table 5.6 specifies the tendencies of an effective negotiator. These are behavioural tendencies, not hard-and-fast rules of behaviour; exceptions are always possible. The table also shows a profile of a naïve negotiator.

It all boils down to the fact that one must be able to recognize the different types of negotiating activities and to use them independently of one another. It is as simple as that! They tend to 'contaminate' one another in a naïve negotiator. If he takes a tough stance on the content, then he will also tend to act irritated and to sulk, he will want to score points, he will behave rather rigidly and stick to one track. His tough standpoint will come across as even tougher than strictly necessary. A negotiator who knows how to keep the four dimensions separate will evoke less resistance and make a much more reasonable impression (which, of course, he does). And yet he is not a bit more yielding than his 'tough' colleague: he is often even tougher. He concentrates his tenacity on his ultimate goal: a tangible compromise which is as advantageous as possible for him. He is aware that mutual dependency can benefit *both* parties. He is also aware of the fact that it is in his own interests to influence relations positively for the sake of the continuity of the relationship.

Three final remarks

1. A *constituency* means additional problems. People can have constituencies in organizations: *their* division, department or team negotiates along with them. It is important to see the relationship with the constituency as a negotiating relation, too, in order to have a little elbow-room.

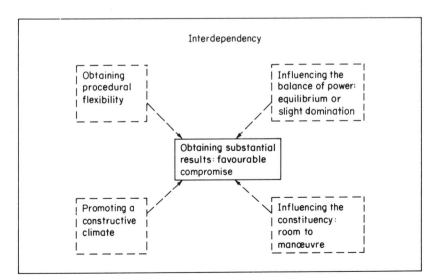

Figure 5.1   Elements of negotiating model

2. Figure 5.1 summarizes the main elements of the model of negotiating described here. The background of all these elements is *interdependency*. This means that all the elements are influenced by the interdependency. At the negotiating table, people try to alter others perception of it: these are the activities aimed at altering the balance of power.
3. It can be useful for negotiators to make a conscious division into several *phases*. Negotiating phases were described above as a procedural technique to improve flexibility. Briefly summarized: (a) start with a *diagnosis* of mutual premises and interests; investigate where interests overlap and keep an eye on the priorities on both sides. Scanning other options and *alternatives* is also part of this; (b) introducing a very broad 'platform proposal' is often an effective procedural step; the proposal can serve as an outline for (c) *amendment and alteration* until a compromise is reached. Using these phases can help to prevent the situation from developing into hostile arguments about positions.

5.3   THEORETICAL AND PRACTICAL IMPLICATIONS

Two matters concerning negotiating are of extreme interest in the context of this study. Theoretically, it forces us to take into consideration the mixed nature of relations. It is very obvious that *both* the interdependency *and* the individual interests are prominent. Practically, negotiating offers interesting possibilities for interventions in organizations.

Theoretical implications

Theoretically speaking, negotiating is difficult to grasp because of its mixed-motive nature. One of the most important theoretical works on negotiating is that by Walton and McKersie (1965). It is thought-provoking to see their struggle with the mixed-motive nature of negotiation. They distinguished: (1) *distributive bargaining*, directed at maximizing one's share of substantial benefits; (2) *integrative bargaining*, directed at problem-solving and the increase of mutual benefits; (3) *attitudinal structuring*, or attempting to create a good working relationship; and (4) *intra-organizational bargaining*, directed at influencing team mates and constituents.

In this chapter attitudinal structuring has been incorporated as 'promoting a constructive climate'. Influencing the balance of power is of such central importance as to merit a place as a separate activity. Distributive and integrative bargaining have been replaced by other categories. This distinction clouds one of the most essential characteristics of negotiating: *negotiating is both distributive and integrative*. Walton and McKersie seemed to be aware of this when they introduced a fifth type of activity: *mixed bargaining*. In a later publication Walton (1972, p. 104) tried to eliminate mixed negotiating by recommending separation of the distributive and integrative elements (e.g. other negotiators, another date, another place). This seems an awkward solution. We have stressed the simultaneity of conflicting interests and mutual dependencies as a central characteristic. Negotiating is a kind of balancing act. Effective negotiators know how to combine self-interests with interdependencies. We have repeatedly seen that these seeming paradoxes are perfectly normal in relations within organizations. Having some knowledge about negotiating heightens our attention to people's abilities to cope with such situations and to find a way out that minimizes the chance of a violent conflict.

Practical implications

The insights into negotiating as they have been presented in this chapter do not take into specific consideration the approach of organizational consultants. It will be discussed in this section and in the following cases. In consultancy, negotiating is of great importance in at least two ways:

1. Training people in negotiating techniques;
2. Utilizing negotiation in specific interventions.

After a discussion of these two practical implications, the chapter will be concluded with a few illustrations.

1. Training people in negotiating techniques

Developing the negotiating skills of organization members can be an important contribution to the regulation of conflict. It is an alternative to the sometimes forcible attempt to fit organization members into a co-operative model. If openness and trust are not easily attainable, this by no means needs to lead to unhealthy personal relations or to a destructive atmosphere. Negotiating can prevent destructive tendencies. Mutual respect is still possible. It can even be challenging and motivating.

Here lies what I like to call *the paradox of co-operation*: if, in situations of somewhat contrasting interests, one decides to co-operate in openness and trust, one may increase the chance of destructive conflicts! There are examples in which a party thinks he can make negotiations take a smooth and amicable course by making a generous proposal at the outset. What happens is that the other party quickly rakes in its profits and then sits down to negotiate. Naturally, the negotiations become extremely arduous because one of the parties feels thoroughly deceived. Fairness, or the notion that if one adopts a co-operative attitude, the other side will do so as well, is untenable here. On the contrary, there is a tendency to see it as necessary yielding, or as weak and inept. It evokes exploitative and competitive behaviour; in the long run it promotes resistance and revenge. So an attempt to introduce a co-operative model in situations of contrasting interests can turn out to be destructive.

Consultants working on management development programmes can be too one-sided about this as well. Openness, self-actualization and a participative style are often prominent. This is not to say that these skills and insights cannot be of great importance. By no means! But they must not be advocated with the implication that ultimately everyone in the organization can and should work towards them in all situations. They are most effective in situations of high interdependence and strong common interests.

Training in negotiating techniques: several examples

1. The regional offices of a banking firm became more autonomous. New systems brought the results of the individual branches into clearer view. Increasing competition for interesting clients in 'one another's regions' was the result. In addition, it led to a more independent attitude towards the head office. This development was also encouraged by the use of transfer pricing for the assistance and support from central staff departments.

   Polarized relations and delayed decision-making were foreseen. Several days were devoted to conferences to teach negotiating skills for such situations. Simulations were used of practical situations of two types of frequently occurring contrasts: (a) region vs region; (b) region vs head office.

2. Managers of profit centres of a retail company had a hard time finding a good basis for co-operation both in the stores and among themselves. Purchasing and sales had recently been combined; the new department was jointly responsible for the results. But classic frictions between purchasing and sales were still playing a role. The profit centres competed for budgets, space and other facilities. In a series of workshops, the problems were defined and negotiating skills were taught to resolve them.

3. Administrators of a large professional organization observed that negotiations with other interest groups, including government authorities, were becoming more and more tedious. Internal bickering was increasing. It took more and more effort to get the divergent interests inside the association under a common denominator. A third complication was the fact that the constituencies were growing more active. In several two-day conferences negotiating skills were taught and applied to specific situations.

4. A great many struggles for competence occur within and among some Dutch governmental agencies. Decisions are split up over a large number of authorities, each of which only oversees a single aspect of the problem. This is not very conducive to a smooth work flow or co-ordination. An attempt is being made to reach optimal solutions and workable compromises faster by teaching negotiating skills.

2. Utilizing negotiation in specific interventions

Very *specific interventions* can be deduced from a knowledge of negotiating.

Examples

1. Not striving for the *best* solution based on extensive research, but fairly quickly introducing a tentative proposal and using it as an outline for a compromise among the parties;
2. Being able to chair negotiations between parties;
3. Being able to see impasses and crises as natural and sometimes even as constructive;
4. Not defending the opinion, the report or the solution of the consultant but inviting parties to formulate the conditions on the basis of which they can agree;
5. Having a sense for constituency problems, helping to 'sell' the results;
6. Restricting parties' opportunities to continue arguing, knowing how to turn the discussion to concrete proposals or conditions;
7. At a certain point, actively seeking the role of intermediary in the awareness that parties sometimes more easily make concessions to a third party than to their opponent;
8. If matters become deadlocked, having parties enumerate the consequences of *not* reaching an agreement.

In short, recognizing a situation as a negotiating situation means that the consultant makes use of a different style from when he tries to improve the socio-emotional climate or strives for a well-ordered decision-making process. To conclude this chapter, we will illustrate this with a description of a case in which the consultant switched to a negotiating perspective at a certain point.

In a central works council, disagreement arose among the elected members from the various plants about the allocation of new jobs over the plants. According to a management plan, there was one plant which could count on expansion. Two other plants would have to give up jobs. Disagreement on this escalated so high that even fairly simple matters became contentious issues. Mistrust grew. Sharp reproaches and emotional accusations became the order of the day.

The consultant decided to use an approach advocated by Blake, Schepard and Mouton (1964): holding a confrontation meeting to reduce mistrust, and then using a problem-solving model to tackle the question it all started with. The confrontation meeting took one day. Afterwards, people had mixed feelings about the result. Some of them called it a waste of time and wanted to get down to 'business'. For others, things had been cleared up. According to the consultant, not much had changed. The mistrust hardly seemed less, only the intensity of the conflict had been reduced. This was due in part to an agreement about a cooling-off period during which the parties were not to undertake any further action in the matter.

The next session lasted two and a half days. The consultant started by explaining the problem-solving model, which would be the method of working for the rest of the conference. After a constructive start, on the morning of the second day the matter was completely deadlocked. Two diametrically opposed standpoints were at odds. The problem-solving model no longer worked, parties merely repeated their standpoints. The atmosphere rapidly worsened. Personal attacks and emotional accusations started. The consultant decided to leave the problem-solving model for what it was. He adjourned the meeting and asked the factions to consult among themselves on the crisis that had come about, particularly about the possible *consequences* if it were to continue.

The consultant had been groping in the wrong direction, but here he started to find the right tack. At issue was the distribution of scarce resources—jobs. From then onwards, his approach focused more and more on getting the parties to negotiate. Clinging to the *crisis* was a strong intervention; instead of worrying about a failure of the talks and undertaking an industrious search for compromises, he did something entirely different.

He had the parties investigate *the consequences of a lasting crisis*: a meeting prematurely broken off, continuing combat, animosity, resignation of several members, greatly decreased credibility of the elected members among their constituents, impaired influence on the management, etc. People were impressed by this and decided to try once more. The consultant asked the parties to set down conditions on the basis of which they could agree to a rough draft of a compromise. *This use of a proposal as a platform for negotiations was decisive for the further course of the conference.* The 'platform proposal' could be altered and amended in all possible ways. It put a stop to the endless arguments. All energy was concentrated on working out a concrete proposal. The consultant viewed the impasses occurring after this in the discussions (actually negotiations) as legitimate pressure on one another's standpoints. He allowed them to continue until, generally after an adjournment, a concession set things in motion once again. In short, he worked with a typical negotiation approach. Ultimately the parties reached a compromise.

This case clearly illustrates the importance of the distinction between instrumental relations and negotiating relations. For instance, to regulate work-flow interdependencies better in a department, a problem-solving approach may provide the necessary leverage. But in the distribution of the scarce resource, jobs, a different approach is called for—negotiating. And naturally one might wonder if the confrontation meeting, a typical socio-emotional intervention, was really necessary in this case.

In order to develop the appropriate style during a process such as this, precise knowledge is required of what normally takes place during negotiations and what behaviour is constructive.

6 Instrumental and Socio-emotional Relations

6.1 INTRODUCTION

Two of the four types of relations, power relations and negotiating relations, have been discussed at length. In Section 6.2 we will cover the two other types of relations and the interventions appropriate to them. Section 6.3 will describe a case which demonstrates the usefulness of our distinction into several relational aspects.

Since this will complete our treatment of the four relational aspects, it is also a good opportunity to review them from two points of view. In Section 6.4 we will discuss the fact that reality may be so complex as to render it impossible to diagnose organizational problems equivocally. In Section 6.5 we will investigate the role of the four relational aspects in the relationship between consultant and client.

6.2 BEHAVIOURAL TENDENCIES, PROBLEMS AND INTERVENTIONS

The model of organizations as several parties competing for power is one-sided. Pfeffer (1978, p. 181) expressed this as follows: 'The contest over organisational structures represents a contest for control of the organisation. Yet this contest for power is not unbounded. Constraints on the struggle for control are imposed by the mutual interdependence of the parties involved. After all, the essence of organisations is interdependence among the interacting groups.'

Parties are linked to one another by a multitude of interdependencies from which all of them stand to gain. But organizations do not consist merely of these. Units in organizations have self-interests and are dependent on one another at the same time. Competition and co-operation occur simultaneously. Depending on the situation, different aspects may receive more emphasis. Sometimes relations are characterized by very strong mutual dependencies, sometimes by almost mutually exclusive interests. Mutual dependency and co-operation are prominent in instrumental and socio-emotional relations. We can look at the way in which those involved deal with these relations in the same way as we did for power and negotiating relations:

1. Behavioural tendencies: what sort of behaviour do those involved tend to exhibit?
2. What problems can occur, what sorts of frictions are to be expected?
3. What interventions are appropriate to these problems?

We will elaborate on these three points for the two remaining types of relations.

Confusion can arise about what is meant by behavioural tendencies in this context. The term is used here to refer to the behaviour those involved exhibit in dealing with their mutual relations and the inevitable frictions that occur in them. The difficulty here is that it is sometimes hard to separate *description from prescription*. This behaviour is constantly evolving, sometimes influenced by the many authors who propagate a wide variety of insights and techniques using conferences, training, management development programmes, etc. Is it possible that prescription can thus become reality?

We must be careful that normative considerations do not take on too great a role. The instrumental approach, for example, is all too often applied in matters that are primarily characterized by power relations (see p. 114). On p. 125 I cited Schutz who thought world problems could be solved among government leaders by means of a typical socio-emotional intervention, the encounter lab. More examples could be given of a particular approach, which may work very well in some situations, becoming the norm for many other sorts of situations. The qualities of an approach are superimposed on other sorts of relations.

In addition, our knowledge about specific relations is sometimes inadequate. Extensive literature about problem-solving and decision-making is available in the task-oriented, instrumental field. But the model of successive phrases in decision-making described in this literature has hardly any empirical foundation. 'It is striking that authors who were not content with merely taking over this model, but who investigated how these decision making processes actually went, were unable to discover the phases the model indicates' (Bos, 1974, p. 54). 'Studies of the applicability of such models indicated that their effect on the actual manner of decision-making in organisations is slight and is primarily limited to routine operational decisions' (Koopman, 1975, p. 39). Individual case studies such as those of Cyert, Dill and March (1958) and especially the empirical work of Mintzberg, Raising-hani and Théorêt (1976) have given us several drastic adaptations of this phase model. But in this work prescriptive levers in the form of convenient models and concrete skills can scarcely be found.

So it may seem as if we are swung back and forth between prescriptive theories that do not accommodate reality and empirically founded insights with which we can do little in practice. An exception is the work by Bos (1974) which replaces the phase model by a model based on rhythm and polarity. On the face of it, it sounds complicated, because we are less familiar in our thinking with these sorts of concepts than with the straightforward idea of successive phases. And yet Bos's model is readily recognizable and applicable. In a certain sense, his model integrates the phase model. At any rate, it makes redundant an auxiliary construction that is necessary to save the phase model. I am referring to the idea that the series of phases repeats itself in short cycles. This iterative element probably brings the phase model closer to reality, but much of the prescriptive value is lost in the process. The straightforward and logical succession becomes much more of a jumble. Bos nevertheless managed to impose some order on it.

Despite the amount of work that has been done in various fields, it is in fact a tedious business to arrive at useful and well-founded insights. It is very easy to lose track of the whole in considerations that have little or nothing to do with observable phenomena, in this case our need for normative foundations or for familiar frames of thought.

Instrumental relations

Instrumental relations in organizations have traditionally been the focus of much attention. They concern the way in which work and tasks are organized: setting goals, allocating resources, determining the structure and defining procedures.

Division of labour and specialization make workers more and more dependent on one another. People can no longer produce anything without co-ordinating their work with that of a growing number of others. This makes the problems of throughput and co-ordination central. We can make many subdivisions in these work-oriented types of interdependencies such as work flow, planning, control and communication. People who deal with these types of relations tend to fairly rational behaviour such as collecting information, setting down criteria which a solution must meet, comparing alternative solutions. They welcome the use of quantitative data and methods.

This aspect is chiefly rational. Functional criteria such as internal efficiency or external competitiveness have priority. People are task-oriented. This makes a certain rationality in their viewpoints likely and also effective. 'A certain' rationality, because we often content ourselves with a satisfactory solution which will do for a while. In Simon's (1957) terms, often 'maximizing' is not our aim but rather 'satisficing'. And then we have to make do with a 'bounded rationality' (see also Mintzberg, Raisinghani and Théorêt, 1976).

The point here is that interaction between people is of a different nature from that when power positions or scarce resources are at stake. As March and Simon (1958) put it, here lies the distinction between 'bargaining' and 'politics' on the one hand and 'problem-solving' and 'persuasion' on the other. In this context, Butler et al. (1979) emphasized 'task considerations' and 'power considerations' as the two most important factors that can influence decision-making behaviour—obviously, in opposite directions.

Problems in this area are factual and task-oriented: they are sooner seen as 'logical' than 'political'. Those concerned direct their behaviour accordingly (Shull, Delbecq and Cummings, 1970; Thompson, 1964; Thompson and Tuden, 1959; Veeren, 1978). Problems can take on many forms: unclear priorities or insufficient consensus about priorities, misunderstanding one another, speaking different languages, inadequate communicative skills, clumsy procedures for tackling problems, insufficient exchange of ideas, poor synchronization, unclear division of tasks, a defective co-ordinating structure.

Interventions are of a rational problem-solving nature. Sometimes they are in the form of factual recommendations or solutions given by an expert. Sometimes the aim is to convey insights and methods that facilitate a search for solutions in the area of goals and means, task co-ordination and synchronization (Kepner and Tregoe, 1965; Maier, 1963).

Furthermore, consultants can be more procedurally oriented and recommend a particular systematic problem-solving model as the way in which the matter should be tackled (Drucker, 1963). They can play a role in the various steps of such a model: collecting information, formulating the problem, or developing alternative solutions. Depending on the type of problem, consultants can use more specific procedures such as the strength/weakness analysis or the confrontation meeting of Beckhard for establishing goals, or the job expectation technique and the role analysis technique (Huse, 1980; French and Bell, 1984) for task co-ordination problems.

Socio-emotional relations

The human relations movement with its focus on the informal organization drew attention to the socio-emotional side of relations. People in organizations become attached to one another on the basis of personal likes, the same norms and values, similar identification objects, etc. These effective ties can bring about a very strong 'we-feeling'. The informal groups that thus arise often mean more to people than the formal work relations. The behaviour to which people tend in these situations can be clearly differentiated from the rational behaviour discussed above. In a certain sense it is even *irrational*. This is where people tend to *show their feelings*. Spontaneity, openness, mutual trust and personal interest can more readily be expressed in behaviour. People are also *sensitive to shared identities*. They will use practically everything for this—clothing, terminology, symbols—as long as it strengthens their feelings of belongingness. A firm or organization can sometimes provide its employees with such an identity by means of a colourful tradition, a compelling house style or prestigious achievements.

Problems occur in this field when the personal or collective identity is challenged. These problems are emotionally charged. They relate to self-images, the opinions and prejudices associated with them, and to questions of acceptance and trust. Feelings of commitment to and identification with certain groups, organizations and symbols are at issue, as well as the value systems people hold. Problems may also involve the manner of coping with personal relations. Then they are about the way in which people approach and react to one another. This can go along with strong negative feelings, mistrust and stereotyping.

Interventions. It is interesting how after the Second World War, with the rise of laboratory training and organizational development, these relations were long seen as central. They had to be made manifest and developed in all possible ways. Feedback sessions, sensitivity training and encounter groups became routine interventions (Beckhard, 1969; Bradford, Gibb and Benne, 1964; Miles, 1981; Schein and Bennis, 1965). Enthusiasm for an intervention strategy exclusively aimed at socio-emotional relations is clearly waning (Bradford, 1974).*

But these interventions can be very useful in come cases, such as in conflicts between persons or groups in which mutual distruct and stereotyping loom large, or in team development in a group of highly interdependent persons. In such cases, consultants aim at systematically building up mutual trust and acceptance and at increasing each person's capacity to discuss and to influence the individual functioning of the others (Johnson, 1967, 1972; Johnson and Dustin, 1970). This is also a subject of training in management development.

The two previously discussed groups of interventions are sometimes applied in combination. Generally emphasis is first placed on the socio-emotional side. Later the focus is on the instrumental aspect: how can we increase effectiveness? Examples are the confrontation meeting of Blake and Mouton, grid OD and 'organizational mirroring' (Huse, 1980; French and Bell, 1984).

Both types of relations are found in practical theories on leadership. The *distinction between task and socio-emotional orientation* appears in this context in many variations. Again and again it is emphasized that both aspects demand separate attention. The manner in which this attention is given requires different behaviour on the part of a manager.

In conclusion we may state that much is already known about the occurr-

---

* This is not to say that no more important developments are possible in this field. Until now our work here has been fairly one-sided. Organizational development once primarily aimed at 'showing feelings' and openness between people. The sometimes painful learning processes that thus ensued were termed 'personal growth'. And yet even in this so thoroughly explored field we are still searching for effective interventions for individual dysfunctions. Organizational change may get stuck on certain individuals. An almost therapeutic approach may sometimes be needed to help people back on the rails or to remove inhibitions and disturbances in their functioning. We are little at home in this area.

The second socio-emotional area, that of identification and solidarity, we ignored until a few years ago. What is involved in ordering organizations in such a way that the chances of a satisfying shared identity increase has only started to delineate itself in recent years.

Table 6.1   Instrumental and socio-emotional relations

Sorts of relations	Sorts of problems	Effective strategies of those involved	Interventions by consultants
Instrumental relations	Establishing goals and means, poor co-ordination and synchronization	Rational/technical approach: problem analysis, more efficient meeting and decision-making behaviour, improving planning, providing for clearer division of tasks	Suggesting techniques of problem analysis and decision-making, introducing better co-ordination and planning procedures
Socio-emotional relations	Lack of trust and acceptance, personal irritations, stereotyping	Expressing 'irrational' feelings and irritations, 'talking things out', putting oneself in the other's place	Making irritations and stereotypes open for discussion, training in open communication
	Insufficient opportunities for identification with the organization	A particular house style, selection of personnel with the same 'style'	Developing the mission of the organization

ence and the resolution of problems in these two types of relations. Table 6.1 summarizes what we have discussed thus far.

6.3   CASE

An example will clarify how instrumental problems can be resolved. Most consultants are familiar with the instrumental approach. The commentary on the case will illustrate that such a method is only applicable to a certain type of problem.

Description

A personnel department of a large organization was faced by numerous new tasks in the field of promotion, hiring and dismissal policy, personnel planning, evaluation, job classification and quality development. The company sent more and more of its personnel to training courses so they could hold efficient progress and planning meetings and oversee changes in the organization. It was difficult to keep track of the rapid succession of renewals. The familiar division of tasks was in disarray. The work grew by leaps and bounds, which led to an expansion of the personnel department with academic personnel. This gave rise to adjustment problems, primarily in relations between officials who had learned the trade in practice and new staff members who had been trained in social sciences. The personnel manager became a regular participant in policy deliberations of the top management. This along with the other problems caused the personnel manager to become over-worked. He enlisted a consultant to 'do something about the problem'.

After orientation talks with the personnel manager and a few other officials, at the consultant's suggestion, a meeting was called of the personnel manager and the management level directly under him, the head of the personnel department, the head of personnel evaluation, the firm's social worker, the adjunct personnel manager, the officials for schooling, training and supervision and the official charged with personnel planning. Such a meeting was not at all customary. The personnel manager took care of everything in individual contacts with all of them, and otherwise 'people dropped into each other's offices to take care of things'.

At this first meeting, the consultant suggested that they start out by making an inventory of the difficulties. Problems were written down on wall charts and then ordered. Three clusters became apparent:

(a) The structure of the personnel service. Where do authorities and com-petencies lie, what sort of organization do we want the personnel service to have, how will we co-ordinate responsibilities?
(b) Planning the task performance. What tasks are there, who will do what, what is expected of us, what do we want ourselves?
(c) Co-ordination and consultation. We see one another too little, the personnel manager is often not available, too many things are left undone, we are not in control of things.

Several meetings were held to try to solve these matters, with the consultant acting as chairman. He used a problem-solving model as a guide-line:

1. Forming an overview: inventorying ideas, opinions, information;
2. Generating alternative solutions;
3. Comparing the most important alternatives as to their consequences;
4. Selection;
5. Making agreements about carrying them out.

The problem-solving model was the consultant's way of sticking to the theme. He made practical suggestions for solutions to certain questions. His know-ledge of the problems in other personnel services and preliminary talks with the participants in the meetings had given him a good idea of what would be workable agreements in this situation. Relations between the new employees and the old hands were talked over and set down on paper.

Agreements were made over one question after another. The consultant's role gradually became a more modest one. The personnel manager took the reins. One important decision was to hold such meetings regularly. Communi-cation with the other officials was also improved through periodic consulta-tion.

Commentary

Good work by the consultant. The instrumental approach to the problems turned out to be effective. For many consultants, a method which starts with an inventory of the problems and then seeks to solve them by means of improved communication and clear agreements about tasks and procedures is a kind of routine. In addition, it is a method which management will recognize, and it can count on their approval. But in some cases this method is much less appropriate. Particularly for problems that are related to power relations, it can be far wide of the mark. Etzioni (1964) gave an amusing example:

> In a typical Human Relations training movie we see a happy factory in which the wheels hum steadily and the workers rhythmically serve the machines with smiles on their faces. A truck arrives and unloads large crates containing new machines. A dark type with long sideburns who sweeps the floors in the factory spreads a rumor that mass firing is imminent since the new machines will take over the work of many workers. The wheels turn slower, and the workers are sad. In the evening they carry their gloom to their suburban homes. The next morning the reassuring voice of their boss comes over the inter-com. He tells them that the rumor is absolutely false; the machines are to be set up in a new wing and more workers will be hired since the factory is expanding its production. Everybody sighs in relief, smiles return, the machines hum speedily and steadily again. Only the dark floor sweeper is sad. Nobody will listen to his rumours any more. The moral is clear: had management been careful to communicate its development plans to its workers, the crisis would have been averted. Once it occurred, increase in communication eliminated it like magic.

Rubbish, of course. Imagine eliminating the high vs low dynamic over the intercom! Etzioni rightly stated: 'Differences in economic interests and power positions cannot be communicated away.'

Baldridge (1971, p. 200) called this the 'communication fallacy': reducing problems to misunderstandings that can be resolved by improving communication. The example illustrates how consultants can make mistakes if they reduce problems to one particular type. This book shows how to develop a perspective which offers several interrelated views.

6.4   THE FOUR RELATIONAL ASPECTS AND COMPLEX REALITY

Now that we have treated the four relational aspects, it is a good idea to consider a possible complication. We have discussed each relational aspect as follows:

1. The nature of the relational aspect: on what the interdependency is based.

2. Behavioural tendencies.
3. Dynamics: recurring problems.

We were primarily looking for indications that the relational aspects were associated with problematic behaviour and obvious difficulties in organizations.

But it is an illusion to think that every problem in an organization can be speedily and unambiguously diagnosed and an intervention prescribed. Differences in interpretation are always possible.

The analysis of behavioural tendencies and central problems in the three prototypes in Chapter 4 showed that, for power and dependency relations, the associations are fairly clear. A summary can be found in Table 4.4. Structural problems can only be resolved or eliminated by interventions in the power and dependency aspect. This generally is a laborious process. And there is no structure without problems. This is not to say that altering power and dependency relations should be avoided. There can be good grounds for changing a configuration, such as to bring an ailing high vs low relation more into equilibrium, or to call a halt to an out of control equal vs equal relation by introducing a power centre.

The other relational aspects do not show such a strong association between behavioural tendencies and problems. There are problems aplenty, but they are less ingrained. They are more due to a lack of knowledge and skills, to wrong choices and to the awkward ways people sometimes have of dealing with a relation. These are all things that can be overcome without structural interventions. In such cases a consultant will more likely want to *solve* the problems, while in the former case he is more likely to aim at *regulating or conditioning* them. No absolute lines of demarcation can be drawn between the four sorts of relations nor between two categories of problems: those that can be solved and those that have to be conditioned or regulated. There are some problem and intervention areas in which it is not easy for consultants to reach a consensus about what is wrong and how it should be fixed. These may be very legitimate differences of opinion. It is a matter of what perspective you take.

Ingrained network problems can even be seen as 'frictions' which are relatively easy to tackle, and some manifestations of them can be rectified. Often they are problems in which several aspects play a role simultaneously. Examples are given in Table 6.2. For each of the three prototypes, the first column labels the problem as seen from the power aspect. In the next three columns the same problem or a related problem is viewed from the other three relational aspects. Each column also gives examples of interventions appropriate to the problems.

So on the intervention side, too, it is difficult to separate the four types of relations entirely into a single and clear-cut approach to problems. Human relations are *simultaneously* characterized by power, task dependency, socio-emotional ties and interdependency in the allocation of available

Table 6.2 Examples of different perspectives on the three network problems

	Power aspect	Relational aspect		
		Negotiating aspect	Instrumental aspect	Socio-emotional aspect
Problem:	*Suboptimization*, covert fighting	The sum of all claims exceeds what is available	Frictions in border areas	Irritated personal relations
Intervention:	Activate power centre, integrate or separate parties	Seek common interest, negotiate	Improve co-ordination and communication	Increase mutual trust and acceptance
Problem:	*Control vs autonomy*	'Low' wants a larger piece of the pie	'Resistance to change' vs 'our view is not important'	Arrogance vs apathy or aggression
Intervention:	Structural changes	Negotiate via representatives	Co-determination and participation; better communication	Different style of leadership
Problem:	*Role conflict*	More powers with respect to budgets	Unclearness in tasks	Stress
Intervention:	Vertical task expansion, provide more sanctions and rewards	Assertive behaviour	Improve communication, management by objectives	Talk out problems, stop buffering, start co-ordinating

resources. People and groups in organizations try to strengthen their positions, but at the same time they work together. They influence personal relations while doing their best to secure a goodly share of the available resources. Problems will often be 'mixed', so severul different methods can be applied. This is no cause for concern. The several connotations can be a reflection of reality and they are to be preferred to dogmatically clinging to only one perspective. The same problem—that we can distinguish but cannot always clearly differentiate—was treated in Chapter 2 in terms of organization theory. There, too, we saw this overlapping, mixing and influencing within and between sorts of relations. The practice of consultancy will have to take account of complications in this field. To decrease the *chance* of confusion, in the previous chapters we have tried to indicate as clearly as possible what points should be emphasized for different groups of interventions. *In conclusion*, we may state in all simplicity:

(a) many problems can be better understood by placing them in the model of the four relational aspects;
(b) if ways of arriving at a solution are apparent, by all means do so!
(c) if this is not possible, then better regulation should be attempted;
(d) for serious and chronic problems, structural adaptations of the power and dependency relations may be necessary.

6.5   THE CONSULTANT AS A PARTY IN THE NETWORK

The relation of a consultant to the client organization can also be placed in this model of four types of relations. A consultant can be regarded as one of the parties in the network. His relation to the other parties can be viewed in terms of power, task dependency, affective charge and negotiating position. His behaviour can be more or less efficacious in regulating the tensions in this relation. A wide variety of strategies are available to both parties, and certainly not only co-operative strategies!

We will now briefly describe the four types of relations as they apply to external advisers. Examples will be given of the strategies that consultants use in dealing with these relations.

1. Consultants are enlisted to solve problems. This imparts to the consultant–client relationship a highly developed instrumental aspect. The client has a problem and expects the consultant will have the expertise to find a way out. The consultant is tried and assessed on his expertise. His specialized knowledge and experience are important. Another important factor is how the consultant conducts himself towards the client in this instrumental relation. Does he ask the right questions? Does he quickly demonstrate that he oversees and understands the problem? Do his ideas and suggestions strike at the heart of the problem? Does he see a solution in sight? Often a report which gives a clear analysis of the situation as well

as several realistic recommendations is the criterion by which the consultant is judged on the instrumental aspect.

Working together smoothly, exchanging information, being open to the client's problems—generally speaking, co-operative strategies—come naturally here. *At the same time*, the consulting relationship in all its instrumentality means authority of the consultant and dependency on the part of the client. After all, the adviser was enlisted because the client could not solve the problem himself. Clients generally have some difficulty accepting this, and try not to allow their dependency to affect the balance of power too much.

2. The socio-emotional aspect of the relationship is undoubtedly of great importance. How accepted is the consultant as a person? Does he manage to create a satisfactory atmosphere? In order to influence personal relations in a positive sense, it is important to be able to listen, have a sense of humour, be open and frank, take an interest in the personal side of the matter and not to hold very different norms and values.

   It is unlikely that the socio-emotional aspect will be affected only by personal affinities. Some negative feelings now and then are inevitable. This makes no difference as long as the balance of positive and negative effects comprises enough mutual acceptance to ensure a workable relationship.

3. The negotiating side of the relationship also plays a role. Acquisition, continuity of the project or even a larger project are sometimes very important to the consultant. The market facet is an important aspect of the job of an external consultant which influences many of his decisions, but there are not many references to this in the literature. The market facet does not automatically serve the interests of the client, especially if the consultant does not have a well-filled portfolio.

There is a chance that frictions will occur in these three relations. For example, the client may feel the consultant's expertise is inadequate, personal relations may become irritated or the client may see a less costly alternative for the consultant's work.

4. The consultant–client relationship can also be viewed in terms of power. In principle, the same three basic prototypes are applicable. Internal advisers will often find themselves in the middle position, sandwiched between management and the rest of the organization. The basic structure of the relationship and recurrent structural problems will have to be assessed for each case separately. For example, advisers in an intermediate position may tend to stress their independence or to fight for autonomy from the management. In my experience, this is often a point of contention. The chance of mistrust and resistance at lower levels in the organization is fairly great. They will not place much faith in statements of independence.

Examining the consultant–client relationship in terms of power is another opportunity to explain our view of power:

1. Power is the most central aspect of relations: it unites the other three dependencies;
2. The balance of power among the parties is a focus of attention and a cause of concern; they use a great many different strategies to influence it;
3. Power relations have a conditioning effect: they may cause recurrent structural tensions between the parties.

And how does this affect the consultant–client relationship? The power balance is largely determined by the consultant's 'score' on the first three relational aspects. A positive or negative mark may be expected on each relational aspect. Their sum total gives an indication of the perceived qualities of the consultant—expertise, personal acceptance and market position. To this is added the skill of consultant and client at the power game, a game with several aspects.

We now want to investigate how the power sources that Pettigrew (1975) considered of special importance to consultants fit in this pattern. Pettigrew mentioned:

1. *Expertise*. This clearly falls under the instrumental dimension of the consultant–client relationship. The greater the consultant's expertise and the less it is common property, the greater is the dependency of the client.
2. *Status*. A consultant can strengthen his position by some manifest and conspicuous successes. By making an educated guess of what will convince the client, a consultant can use 'impression management' to establish his reputation and strengthen his position.
3. *Control of information*. By virtue of his position, a consultant has an informational advantage. He can use it to steer opinion formation. And he can use it against people who thwart his efforts. Even if a consultant would not dream of divulging his knowledge of the organization, the client can never be 100 per cent certain of it.
4. *'Political' intuition and access to the power centres*. We have seen the importance of a 'political' perspective of the organization and good relations with the formal and informal seats of power.
5. *Support from colleagues*. According to Pettigrew, consultants are often on a tense footing with their colleagues, which is a serious handicap for them. In his view, these tensions are so common that clients often tend to enlist several consultants and then to use them against one another, in order to influence the power balance in their own favour.

It is striking that Pettigrew did not mention *personal trust* in this list. Rubinstein (1977), who, broadly speaking, named the same power sources for consultants, did mention it explicitly. Expertise, status, control of information and personal trust fit in the framework of three types of relations: instrumental, socio-emotional and negotiating relations. Expertise and personal trust are self-evident, status has to do with the market position, control of information is a variant of expertise. One fact stands out in the way in which Pettigrew wrote about status as 'impression management', and about the one-sided use of information: there is at least one power strategy that the consultant must master, that of 'selling' himself and his ideas. Exploiting his more objective qualities is merely a transition to the political game. Pettigrew's other power sources clearly accommodate this: insight into political relations, including good relations with the power centres, and no bickering with colleagues and constituencies!

We see that the more political strategies, intended to develop a network which is transparent and receptive to the consultant, one in which he occupies a relatively strong position, are important. But the other relational aspects are also of influence on the power balance.

Table 6.3 summarizes how certain strategies in the various relational aspects can influence the power balance between the consultant and the client.

It would be incorrect to arouse the impression that there is a kind of power struggle between the client and the consultant. There is no power struggle, but there is a fluctuating power balance, one which generally comes into being

Table 6.3   Consultant–client relationship

Relational aspect	Examples of strategies which influence the balance of power	
	Client	Consultant
Instrumental aspect	Giving the consultant opponents. Only enlisting consultant to obtain his knowledge	Pointing out the firm's 'blind spot' to the client. Increasing informational advantage. Flooding with expertise
Socio-emotional aspect	'Taking in' the consultant. Giving 'confidential' information, getting on personal footing with him	'Taking in' the client. Giving 'confidential' information, getting on personal footing
Negotiating aspect	Keeping continuity of job dubious. Developing alternatives for the consultant	Building up strong market position. Having well-stocked order portfolio. Showing client how important and how hard to come by is his special expertise
Power and dependency aspect	Enlisting several consultants and using them against one another. Withholding important information about the political force field	Access to power centres. Insight into the political force field. Forming coalitions, lobbying. Obligating others to him

quickly and unspectacularly, without the consultant having much grasp of it. The reputation of the consultant, the level at which he comes in and the manner in which he presents himself in the initial contacts 'automatically' bring the balance in a certain position.

7 Consulting Approach and Intervention Programmes

7.1 INTRODUCTION

Chapters 4, 5 and 6 covered a large number of problems and interventions. Here we would like to present an integrative framework. The intervention programmes are grounded on the four aspects of relations between units. In the terms of our diagram in Chapter 1, we are talking about the relationship between specific interventions and integrative strategies (Figure 7.1).

This chapter contains a great many indications about how to use the arsenal of interventions we have discussed. It is intended to provide a systematic basis for concrete problems. It thus forms an important complement to the system-wide change strategies described in Chapter 3, where the following three general strategic steps were named:

Step 1. Identifying the problem;
Step 2. Developing 'political' support;
Step 3. Solving the problem using the 'one-in-three model'.

We will work with the same steps, but now our focus will be tensions and conflicts in the relations between units in an organization.

Tension and conflict are the background of many requests for advice. Conflict is defined very broadly here: a manifest impasse, pronounced discontent, a decision-making process grinding to a halt can be included.

In the next section a framework for interventions will be presented based on two points of view: (1) consulting approach; (2) relational aspect. Subsequently an intervention programme will be presented in the form of seven postulates. The first three postulates primarily have to do with the power aspect of relations in the network. The last three postulates are about how a consultant works and the importance of the distinction into different sorts of problems and interventions. The fourth postulate sets down the conflict intensity as a separate variable which can bring about a shift of emphasis in interventions. In the last sections of this chapter, the programme will be worked out more concretely and illustrated with examples.

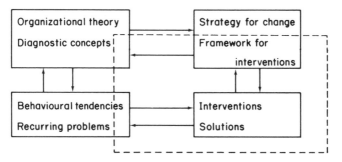

Figure 7.1 Contents of Chapter 7

7.2 FRAMEWORK FOR INTERVENTIONS

For a classification into sorts of problems and conflicts, we will make use of our distinction into relational aspects. It is interesting to see how these aspects are brought up with varying emphases in the classifications of other authors. Walton (1969) distinguished 'substantive issues'—differences about goals and means, competition and scarce resources—from 'emotional issues'—negative feelings between parties. In a later study he spoke of conflicts with instrumental and expressive stakes (Walton, 1972). The latter refers to conflicts in which the identity feelings of the person or group are at issue. Morris and Sashkin (1976) distinguished breakdowns in communication, substantial problems and conflicts based on emotions or values. Robbins (1974) mentioned communication problems, structural factors, including conflicting interests, and clashing personalities.

Here we will use the classification into the four relational aspects treated earlier:*

1. Instrumental conflicts have a business-like and task-oriented content. They can take many forms: unclear priorities or lack of consensus about priorities; misunderstandings, speaking different languages, inadequate communicative skills; clumsy procedures for approaching problems, insufficient exchange and co-ordination of ideas, unclear task division.
2. Socio-emotional conflicts. This type of conflict occurs when a person's identity is at stake. They are emotionally charged. These conflicts are about the image a person has of himself, the opinions and prejudices associated with it and questions of acceptance and trust. Often commitment to and identification with groups, institutes and symbols are at issue, as well as a person's value system. These conflicts can also be concerned with the manner of dealing with personal relations. They are then about

---

* According to the predominant view of organizations, some sorts of conflicts will be considered more important than others. The aspects of conflict correspond to the following views of organisations: (1) the organization as a machine; (2) the organization as a family; (3) the organization as a market; (4) the organization as a pecking order.

the way in which people approach one another and react to one another. This may involve strongly negative feelings.

3. Negotiating conflicts. These involve the tensions that occur in the allocation of scarce resources, which may be almost anything: money, equipment, space, interesting work, secretarial support, automation facilities. It is quite easy for bickering to enter into an allocation question: everyone tries to get a 'reasonable' piece of the cake for his own party.

4. Power and dependency conflicts. These involve the rivalries in an organization which are aimed at safeguarding or strengthening one's strategic position. In 'horizontal' relations we often see it as rivalries for 'responsibility'. Vertical relations typically show tensions such as role conflict, resistance to change and striving for more autonomy vs the need for control.

An important reason for using this classification is that the activities parties must undertake to find a way out are different in each of the four types. This is one of the themes of this book, but other authors use similar distinctions. Walton (1972) proposed negotiating as an effective alternative to problem-solving. In order to cope successfully with the allocation of scarce resources, an arsenal of tactics is needed (Fisher and Ury, 1981; Scott, 1981) fundamentally different from the methods that look for solutions in terms of goals, means, tasks and procedures (Kepner and Tregoe, 1965; Simon, 1960; Drucker, 1963). Variants of problem-solving models developed specially for conflict situations are found in Filley (1975) and Levi and Benjamin (1977).

Conflicts which are emotionally charged demand other strategies, for instance, increasing the capacity for understanding on both sides (Johnson, 1967; Johnson and Dustin, 1970), or systematically building up mutual trust and acceptance. Walton (1965, p. 170) gave a concise description of the tactics suited to this. Power conflicts also demand another approach (Mulder, 1977; Aubert, 1971). But pronounced conflicts in this field are comparatively infrequent. Tensions here tend to stay underground. Power relations do 'colour' other sorts of tensions. They determine the conditions in which tensions are to be resolved by a consultant. The first postulates of the intervention programme make statements about this. The power aspect generally does not determine the contents of the conflict, but it does determine the framework in which it must be solved. It will sometimes be necessary to alter the balance of power before looking to the other aspects of a conflict; for instance, if parties are in constant disagreement about the division of their tasks because of the absence of a central authority.

Effective behaviour appropriate to the four relational aspects has been discussed at length in earlier chapters and is very briefly summarized here. In instrumental questions it is appropriate to look for the best *solution*. In negotiating problems, a *compromise* needs to be reached. In socio-emotional tensions, we should strive for *understanding* on both sides. In power questions we try to achieve *a productive balance between autonomy and dependency*. See also Table 7.1.

Table 7.1   Sorts of conflicts

Sorts of conflict	Effective behaviour	Result
Instrumental conflicts	Problem analysis, efficient meeting and decision-making techniques	Solution
Socio-emotional conflicts	Empathy on both sides, open communication	Understanding
Negotiating conflicts	Negotiating	Compromise
Power conflicts	Structuring mutual dependency	Productive tension

This distinction into sorts of conflict for which different types of solutions are appropriate is important. Confusion and imprecision can arise from the fact that consultants 'believe in' or are accustomed to an approach which has very little in common with the conflict at hand. A telling example is Schutz (1973), who seriously suggested having the presidents of the United States and the Soviet Union solve world problems during an encounter lab. Lakin (1972) gave other examples (police vs citizens; Arabs vs Jews) of resolving conflict by means of training courses which raise some doubts about the adequacy of this particular type of intervention. Many consultants also seek to achieve high-quality solutions by means of thorough research and careful analysis. This tempts the parties into a misleading discussion of his advice and requests for more detailed analysis, while more might have been gained from a compromise proposal to be used as a platform for further negotiations.

A second point of view for a co-ordinating framework for interventions is the *nature of the consulting approach*. In the literature on consulting approaches, the distinction between expert method and process consultation is a common one (Van de Bunt, 1978). The aim of the former is to give a solution to a problem as it is stated by the organization. The consultant investigates matters and comes up with a solution, then sets down his findings in a report which he gives to the client. The focus of the process consultation method is the way in which the client deals with the problem. The consultant acts in an advisory and supportive capacity. He tries to teach the client insights and skills to increase his 'problem-solving capacity'. A third method is the procedural approach (Marx, 1978), in which consultants provide guidance. Here successive steps or phases are distinguished. Consultants try to make the change process manageable by pointing out attainable steps and then defining them concretely with the client.

These points of view can be used to systematize our arsenal of interventions. Examples are given in Table 7.2.

In this survey, the three consulting approaches have different emphases. Traditionally the process approach was chiefly applied to the socio-emotional aspects of relations. Here the process approach is considered to be equally

Table 7.2   Examples of interventions based on different consulting approaches and for different relational aspects

Relational aspects	Expert method	Procedural approach	Process consultation
Power and dependency aspect	Design organizational structure, make (de)centralization plan, have higher echelon intervene, remove intermediate level, develop power base, integrate departments into product/market combinations	Provide phased work plan to bring about structural changes, suggest participation procedures, help parties develop a strategy which will decrease the risk of an escalating power struggle	Clarify the dynamics of power relations, training in coping with power and dependency relations, use role reversal to get across how a 'high vs low' situation works
Instrumental aspect	Co-ordination and planning systems, stock control system, design new sales organization, introduce job classification system, install procedures for quality control	Teach management by objectives, programme to introduce quality circles, team development programme aimed at increasing efficiency, teach techniques of project management	Training in problem-solving and decision-making, make obstacles in relations on the job open to discussion, training in management by objectives
Negotiating aspect	Install budgeting system, work out an investment plan, introduce bonus system, present a compromise in case of frictions about resources	Chair negotiations, suggest phasing and procedures to tackle 'allocation question', help to sell a compromise to the constituency	Training in negotiating technique, assertiveness training, teach parties to negotiate more constructively by simulating real negotiations
Socio-emotional aspect	Make concrete proposals for defining common values and the mission of the organization, define the workings of an organization's culture, design new house style	Provide programme to develop 'corporate identity', provide programme of team development, give rules and procedures for coping with interpersonal conflicts	Training in expressing feelings and irritations, develop mutual acceptance and openness, eliminate mistrust and irritation between departments

applicable to the other relational aspects. The table also shows that we can see relations as the object of expert and procedural interventions. Traditionally, relations have primarily been seen as the object of process consultation. In my view, interventions always have to do with regulating or better structuring relations. To achieve this, we offer solutions, we suggest procedures along which people can find a way out, or we develop people's abilities to find solutions themselves.

The distinction into 'expert, procedural, process' can do no more than point out the main emphasis of a consulting approach. A mixture of different approaches is inevitable. Process consultation, for instance, can be very adequately combined with concrete suggestions for improvement or with a compromise proposal. Another common combination is a draft proposal for concrete changes with a procedure for carrying it out.

The main emphasis of the approach we will describe here is procedural. We do assume that a consultant will proficiently combine this approach with concrete proposals or with process interventions. The approach is intended to provide a more concrete basis for intervening than was given by our description of individual interventions. The framework is complementary in that it provides *added grip*. It supplies a *repertory of interventions* appropriate to four different types of problem areas.

7.3   AN APPROACH TO CONFLICT

Consultancy in conflict situations has yielded a large number of practical ideas. It has made the conditions that contribute to the success of interventions relatively clear. Guide-lines have been developed for a variety of situations:

- conflicts between employers and employees (Blake, Mouton and Sloma, 1965; Margerison and Leary, 1975);
- conflicts between states (Lakin, 1972; Walton, 1970; Burton, 1969);
- conflicts between departments of large organizations (Goodstein and Boyer, 1972; Blake, Shepard and Mouton, 1964);
- interpersonal conflicts (Walton, 1969; Filley, 1975);
- conflicts between races (Chalmers and Cormick, 1971).

What we are aiming at is an orderly and coherent programme. Deutsch (1973) gave the following list of similarities among third-party interventions:

- clarifying the most important issues;
- creating favourable conditions to grapple with the issues;
- improving communication;
- formulating different rules of conflict management;
- helping to find alternative solutions;
- helping to sell the solution.

This gives a few guide-lines for interventions but it is still too vague. Walton (1969) gave a scenario for a productive confrontation that is somewhat more specific and that is more substantive on several points in interventions:

- investigate whether the parties are positively motivated to do something about the conflict;
- try to keep the situational power in balance;
- co-ordinate the confrontation meetings; for instance, a time that suits both

parties, neutral territory, initiative should come from the third party and not from one of those involved;
- alternate differentiation and integration phases; successful integration— resolving the problem—is only possible after elaborate differentiation— exploring specific grievances and opinions of both sides;
- promote conditions that bring about openness;
- promote reliable communication;
- provide for optimal tension in the confrontation situation.

The following summarizes an effective intervention strategy by a third party in the form of *several postulates*. Each postulate marks a pivotal place in the process of conflict management. We might think of them as turning-points where essential intervention choices must be made: whether or not to intervene, what intervention to make, etc.

1. The parties involved in the conflict must accept the third party

This implies that parties must be positively motivated to do something about the conflict and to do so with the help of this particular third party. A good relationship with all parties is very important. If the third party becomes identified with one of the parties, he can no longer do his work.

The following can be of help:

- contacts at an early stage with *both* parties;
- providing *clarity* about how the third party will set to work;
- setting up a '*sounding-board*'; moderate representatives of both parties and a few responsible managers should have seats; they can clarify the intentions of the third party to their constituencies; they can make him aware of important points; this group can also play an important role in subsequent steps; sometimes it will gradually start to play a more substantial role.

If it does not 'click' with one of the parties or if a party sees no point in getting down to work on the conflict, then it is very doubtful whether the third party should go on.

2. The network of conflicting parties must be structured

- A third party must get a clear picture of the structure in the parties.

Some degree of organization in each party is needed. Unclear leadership, internal power struggles, keen rivalry between fractions and other ambiguities form important obstacles to conflict management. If one party shows great internal division and heavy competition, then a third party will first have to achieve some internal consensus. It is very important to become acquainted with the formal and informal leaders. It is not only their opinions which are important to the third party, but also their willingness to participate actively in the process of conflict management. This may mean that a consultant will have to do more than simply discover the structure on both sides. Sometimes he will have to help parties achieve a less ambiguous internal structure; for instance, by suggesting a clear procedure to help them select authoritative spokespersons.

- A third party must structure the relationship between the parties and a co-ordinating central authority.

If there is a central authority, for instance, a higher or more central official, then his co-operation and an active relationship between the consultant and this centre of power will increase the chance of success. Sometimes the problem is a lack of central authority: it is non-existent or it does not exercise its power. In such cases, an important task of the consultant can be developing a power centre to act as a driving force in regulating the conflict.

It is common practice to orient oneself by holding several interviews with the parties. These interviews can yield information about the important points mentioned so far:

- acceptance;
- demarcation and internal structure;
- possible composition of a 'sounding-board'.

They also provide the third party with information about the following critical points we will discuss later:

- intensity;
- symmetry, or a balance of power;
- the nature of the conflict, expressed as substantive problems and grievances.

The sounding-board and the interviews together give the third party the opportunity to develop his *programme of action* while he is exploring the situation. Such a programme sometimes includes preliminary conditions primarily intended to regulate the intensity of the conflict. It often contains a schedule for one or more meetings to tackle the problems, sometimes including procedures for preparatory activities in each party individually.

3. A third party must keep the parties somewhat in equilibrium

Without some symmetry in relations between the parties, a third party cannot work. The very fact that a third party has been called in makes it very likely that there is a certain equilibrium between the parties. For the greater the power differences, the greater is the chance that the more powerful party will settle the conflict by simply imposing its will and forcing the other party to accept it.

My impression is that third parties will primarily step in in impasses and deadlocks in which the parties are more or less a match for each other. In fact, an impasse (or the threat of an impasse because the parties are more or less equal) is the prime mover in studying the nature of the conflict, its consequences and alternative solutions. As parties are generally very keen on maintaining the balance of power, the consultant may not disturb it. Fairly simple matters such as spending approximately equal time on all parties and separate discussions in a neutral location are important.

4. A third party must maintain a certain 'optimal' level of conflict intensity

If the intensity is very high, conflict management becomes impossible. Neither party will show any willingness to communicate with the other. Nor do they see much sense in a third party, particularly if the third party is not unconditionally *against* the other party.

Conflicts which are in a state of very rapid escalation may be out of reach for process consultation. Conflicts can also enter a phase in which the *will to change* is lacking. The parties have more or less learned to live with the conflict. Apparently they prefer the undesired and destructive consequences to another attempt at reaching a compromise with the opponent. The positive self-image is complemented by the negative image of the other. Parties no longer wish to be confronted with other views. It would only stir up doubt. In this way, one can at least uphold one's own definition of a situation in which one has invested so much energy.

These situations are perhaps even harder to deal with than more sudden escalations. Acute crises can sometimes be lulled by introducing a cooling-off period in which the status quo is temporarily maintained.

5. A third party must adapt his interventions to the distinction in four sorts of conflicts

1. Instrumental issues;
2. Socio-emotional trensions and irritations;
3. Questions of allocation;
4. Questions of power.

They are sometimes very intricately intertwined and should then be seen as different aspects of the same conflict. The relationship between aspects and interventions has been discussed at length.

6. A third party must set in motion a repetitive process of differentiation and synthesis

A conflict management process can best be described as a series of activities that sets in motion an ebb and flow of specification and delineation of issues, confrontation of standpoints, and synthesis.

· It is a repetitive process. At each new cycle, a part of the conflict is handled. This can best be done by having both parties work on it. Their grievances are

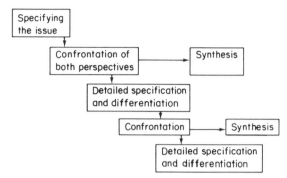

Figure 7.2   Working through an issue

on the table, they are explained, backgrounds and consequences are investigated. A solution is not the immediate goal. The object is to clarify the perspectives of both sides. This confrontation of perspectives will take a different course depending on which aspect is dominant. In instrumental questions, it will primarily be discussion and debate; in socio-emotional issues, putting oneself in the other's place; in questions of allocation, negotiating.

The result of the confrontation of perspectives may be a synthesis: solutions, understanding, compromise. Confrontation can also end in impasses. Impasses compel parties to further specification, again followed by confrontation and so on (see Figure 7.2).

It is quite possible for the processes mentioned in postulates 3, 5, 6 and 7 to take the form of one- or two-day conferences where representatives of the parties involved come together in a more informal atmosphere, with the third party as chairman.

7. The interventions of a third party should be guided by the criteria of directivity, attainability, urgency and movement

An important task of the third party is to provide structure and direction. This demands a forceful and resolute manner. The third party should point out procedures according to which the parties should work. When necessary, he must clarify and defend them. This creates the calm needed to work on the conflict. Vagueness, hesitation and ambiguity create confusion and mistrust. Parties often feel disoriented and somewhat threatened as it is. If a third party is incapable of regulating the interaction between the parties, a hostile atmosphere easily results, making it impossible to debate and discuss, let alone negotiate.

The procedures must translate each subsequent phase into attainable and comprehensible steps. The conflict cannot be handled as a whole because it is composed of several different elements. Which element one chooses depends on where discontent is highest (urgency) but also on how much the parties are capable of. For instance, it is sometimes very difficult to approach socio-emotional conflicts in a strictly business setting. Problems in the other aspects can then take priority because they are easier to manage. A hard-and-fast rule cannot really be given for this. We will have to make do with such guide-lines as:

- consider the climate;
- follow the energy of those directly involved.

It must also be stated that conflict management generally means a large dose of confrontation. The parties often need to be nudged into a confrontation by the third party—so that a third party must often decide to tackle points which the parties tend to avoid. This brings us to the criterion of movement.

Parties in a conflict often show a stereotyped interaction pattern expressed as 'it is too—it is not; you did too—I did not'. Conflict management can easily disintegrate into highly repetitive circular discussions of no added value. A third party must stop such fruitless bickering; progress and movement are essential.

Table 7.3   Summary of the seven postulates about conflict management

Statements	Activities
Developing acceptance	Showing independence, creating clarity
Structuring the network	Clarifying internal structure, structuring relationship between central authority and parties
Promoting equilibrium and symmetry	Dividing attention equally, balancing the parties' influence on the process
Developing optimal intensity	Introducing cooling-off period, pointing out consequences, investigating willingness to change
Distinguishing: • instrumental issues • socio-emotional tensions • questions of allocation • questions of power	Choosing interventions appropriate to this distinction
Specification, confrontation, synthesis	Indicating procedure for specification, confrontation, utilizing impasses for further specification
Being forceful and flexible	Providing clear procedures, putting a stop to circular discussions

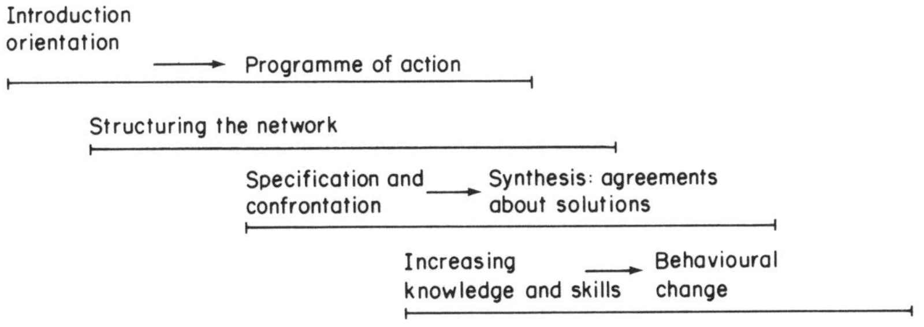

Introduction
orientation
            ⟶   Programme of action
├───┤

        Structuring the network
        ├───┤

                Specification and ___ Synthesis: agreements
                confrontation   about solutions
                ├───┤

                        Increasing   ⟶   Behavioural
                        knowledge and skills   change
                        ├───┤

Figure 7.3   Shift of emphasis in conflict management over time

Summary of the postulates

Table 7.3 briefly recapitulates the postulates.

The order of the postulates here is as much as possible a chronological one. As much as possible, because the activities associated with the postulates show considerable overlap, although some reach a peak at a certain point.

We can summarize how the emphasis of a third party shifts in the course of time schematically as shown in Figure 7.3.

7.4   IMPORTANT CHARACTERISTICS

Here we would like to discuss a few important characteristics of the strategy described: (1) with some adaptations, the strategy is applicable to a wider range of situations than the term 'conflict' might lead us to believe; (2) the strategy is based on a theory of organizations; (3) the strategy combines various consulting approaches.

Scope and applicability

It is important to remark that there are no fundamental differences between the approach described above and an approach to *problems that are not explicitly considered conflicts*. One reason for this is that there is no agreement about what should properly be termed a conflict. A common definition is that used by Van de Vliert (1980): 'Two individuals, an individual and a group, or two groups have a conflict if at least one of the two parties feels that the other party is thwarting or irritating it.' After an unparalleled and extensive survey of all possible definitions, Fink (1968) advocated a very broad definition of conflict. It included, as did Van de Vliert's definition, all kinds of irritations and discord that in common usage would not deserve to be called conflicts. Many people only start to call a situation a conflict if it escalates so openly that it takes on the appearance of an outright fighting situation. Even if a matter is deadlocked, even if there are many contrasts and differences of opinion, people do not readily speak of a conflict. 'Some problems have to be ironed out.' Conflict is a loaded term and this surely plays a role.

The approach as it has been explained here covers the whole range, from mild irritations to escalated confrontations. The common denominator is a network of subunits exhibiting frictions and problems in their relations.

As the intensity increases, it can have a positive effect; it means energy and motivation to do something about the situation. Sometimes a consultant will use interventions to reach this stage (Robbins, 1974; Van de Vliert, 1981a). As long as the intensity is not too high, we need not put much emphasis on the third postulate about symmetry and equilibrium. This means that interventions for more asymmetrical situations (high vs low, high vs middle vs low) described in Chapter 4 are applicable as well.

A situation of very high intensity is characterized by fighting behaviour on both sides. Parties disagree on everything, but above all, each one wants to subjugate the other. In such a case we will have to restrict ourselves to the conditioning factors, or to interventions in the power and dependency relations. Examples: separate parties have a higher echelon impose a binding solution. If it has not escalated so high, sometimes combinations with interventions aimed at the negotiating aspect can be of use: mediating or introducing a 'platform proposal'. A variant which is difficult to deal with occurs when the parties have come to a sort of armed truce. Contact is avoided, the parties have very stereotyped and hostile images of each other. They have learned to live with the situation. Glasl (1980) devoted a great deal of attention to this type of 'cold' conflict.

Organization theory

This approach is based on the theory of organizations described in Chapter 2. According to this theory, the consultant sees things in a 'political' perspective: he tries to localize the strategic positions in the network of interdependent units. His focus is largely the aspect of mutual relations in terms of dependency and power. In this aspect we also find the conditioning factors on which the first three postulates are based. Formulated a little more specifically in terms of power, these three postulates may be stated as follows:

1. A consultant who is not accepted by the parties has an inadequate power base. How can he get the parties to go along with his proposals about how the problems will be approached?
2. Parties must have an internal power structure in order to influence one another. If there are no spokespersons or leaders with influence on their constituency, you have to start from scratch every time.

   In addition, a power centre is important for safeguarding rules and for urging parties to compromise.
3. The consultant must keep the balance of power between parties in equilibrium. If parties are not somewhat in equilibrium, why bother? Is not the outcome already settled?

These conditioning factors determine the chances of success and failure. If the intensity is very high, only interventions associated with the power and dependency aspect can offer any solace. In general, the more chronic the problems he encounters, the more a consultant will consider this type of intervention. He will tend to restructure relations and to develop a pronounced centre of power.

In addition to this aspect, three other aspects can be distinguished in relations between units. This distinction provides a concrete basis to assess the nature of the conflict as well as the appropriate interventions. The conceptual categories of the organization theory are the levers for interventions.

Consulting approach

This approach emphasizes procedural interventions. The consultant adopts a fairly forceful attitude. He points out the procedures to solve the problems and helps in carrying them out. The specification, confrontation and integration process is an important facet of this. At the same time he keeps an eye on the quality of the interaction and tries to improve it if necessary in all four fields by means of process interventions. Sometimes an appeal is made to his mastery of certain subject-matter, for instance, in formulating a better division of tasks.

7.5 EXAMPLES

We will now turn to several specific intervention programmes. These programmes follow the approach described above. This will be explained in a separate part of this section. But they are more concrete and specific. They primarily give indications about the process of specification, confrontation and synthesis. As we will see, it is a process that takes a different form depending on which relational aspect is dominant. In conclusion, we will describe a case showing how consultants influence and utilize the conditioning factors of the power and dependency aspect and combine it with interventions focused on other aspects.

1. Interpersonal conflicts

We will start with a simple type of conflict. The parties are a 'mere' two persons. Their conflict has a strong socio-emotional charge. It is expressed in personal reproaches and increasing bickering about 'small' irritations. The following rules of thumb help a consultant to structure a meeting. The basic idea is that a third party must help them diagnose their conflict. Caught up as they are in the dynamics of continuing polarization, they cannot get out of it on their own.

1. At the start of the meeting briefly relate the history and the intention of the meeting. Possible goals are: to investigate whether some degree of

co-operation can be restored; to talk out how the parties feel about continuing to co-operate; to get some idea of where the trouble lies and whether anything can be done about it.

2. Describe very clearly the procedure to be followed.
   - Take turns in talking about behaviour of the other that irritates you.
   - Do not interrupt.
   - Not until the message of one is clear does the other get the floor.
3. The one who starts must refer to specific behaviour in expressing his irritation or displeasure. The effect this behaviour has on the other person is important.
   'What behaviour does this evoke in the other?'
   Examples?
   Try to describe it.
4. Check whether it is clear to the other.
   'Do you understand what he means?'
   'Can you put it in your own words?'
   'Do you have any idea how this impression was created?'
   'Do you have any idea what behaviour caused this?'
   'What does he want to make clear to you?'

By asking such questions the third party can help a person to allow the message to sink in.

5. If the message is not clear, then the third party can ask the person further questions as under (3):
   'Can you describe it again?'
   'What irritates you the most?'
   'What do you expect of him?'
6. Then give the other the opportunity to express his irritations in the same manner. Again, strive for clarity. Cut off defensive behaviour, rationalizing, excuses, etc.
7. Take your time for this exchange of ideas. Every now and then summarize what behaviours have what effects on both sides. Summarize what the parties apparently want of each other. Ask if your summary is correct.
8. *this may be enough in itself*. Sometimes it is clear that the parties want to continue, that the matter has not yet been cleared up. Then brainstorm about questions such as: 'What might we be able to do about this?'
   'Can each of you imagine behaviour that would probably have this effect but to a lesser extent?'
   'What could you change in your behaviour to evoke a different reaction?'
9. The solution may be to accept the differences and to tolerate a certain amount of tension and irritation. Generally the increased understanding on both sides turns out to be sufficient.
   Try to set down any agreement reached in clear and concrete terms. Make agreements about how long a trial period the parties want; what criteria will be used to assess whether the agreement works. Perhaps you

will make an appointment to meet again to evaluate and adjust the agreement.

The third party must make sure these rules are adhered to fairly strictly, or else the chance of fruitless bickering is great. Basically, the method amounts to increasing the chance that parties put themselves in the other's place to some degree. This makes it primarily applicable to socio-emotional frictions. In its simplest and most reduced form, the approach is: each party gets five minutes to tell what most irritates, grieves or bothers him or her about the other. After that each one repeats the gist of the other's story in his own words!

Conditions

Important to the success of this approach are:

- A certain positive motivation on both sides. Sometimes the parties are so 'burnt out' that there is simply no will to do anything about the conflict.
- The relationship must be somewhat in balance; this means not too great difference in power, neutral location for talks, equal division of the speaking time.
- A preparatory phase in which the third party talks with the parties individually. Then he knows what he can expect, and he can investigate whether both parties are motivated. It gives him an opportunity to prepare the parties by explaining the manner of working which will be used at the joint meeting.

2. Tensions in teams

In this section a few procedures will be explained to be used in team development. An example will be given of a one- or two-day programme.

2.1 Team development meetings

These may focus on instrumental questions. An important aspect of this is exchanging information about tasks and duties and adapting it to one another's views. One way of going about this is having the participants set down for themselves what they see as the most important elements of their tasks: for instance, the two or three priorities they have set themselves for the coming twelve months.

They should set down not only what they expect of themselves, but also the expectations they have with respect to the priorities of their team members. Presenting this in easy view of everyone, for instance on wall charts, is the following step. Then a group discussion can help clarify it. Discrepancies between a person's own priorities and what his team members expect of him are of special importance. Sometimes priorities will have to be adjusted.

This technique has been worked out in several ways. The two best-known variants are the role analysis technique (RAT) by Dayal and Thomas (1968) and the job expectation technique (JET) by Huse and Barebo (1976). JET works as follows:

1. *Find out if JET is attainable.* An orientation phase will show whether both sides feel role clarification is needed. Team members must have the impression that their colleagues and especially their boss will be receptive to such a process of exchange and adjustment.
2. *Set down the objectives.* JET means at least two days of hard work. It takes about three hours to get the job of one team member clear, at least in the original set-up.
3. Find a *quiet location* where you can work without being disturbed.
4. *Description of the job.* The person whose turn it is describes his tasks and responsibilities. He writes them down point for point on a flip-over board. While he is doing this, the others may comment. They say what they agree with and what should be removed. In other words, the whole team contributes to the job description.

   The consultant leads the discussion and is alert to defensive behaviour.
5. When the team members have reached consensus about the description of a certain job, the person himself is responsible for preparing the definitive version. Every participant receives a copy.
6. All the jobs are examined in this way. In general, it is a good idea to start with the 'easiest' jobs and to wind up with the boss.
7. It may be helpful to do JET regularly, say, once a year. JET can be useful in training new team members. It is recommended to go through the JET copies together at a meeting now and then.

Such procedures provide a sound and concrete basis for action. Often a great deal can be achieved with an abridged version. To explain this, we will give an example of a conference which used such a procedure.

2.2 Example of a conference

Duration: one evening, one morning and afternoon. This was a conference of department heads with their plant manager. The object of the meeting was the bickering about unclear division of tasks (instrumental) and more personal tensions (socio-emotional) among team members.

7.00 p.m.   Welcome, objectives, programme.
7.10 p.m.   *Step 1*: task clarification.
Each participant had about 30 minutes to write down, telegram-style, on a flip-over board:
- a short description of his own task;
- most important activities for the upcoming year (his own priorities) (maximum of three items);

- activities of other departments which would help him, which he needed (maximum of three items).

A discussion of each chart followed, primarily of whether expectations of one another were clear on both sides.

11.00 p.m. Closing.

Next day

Morning *Step 2*: tackling mutual tensions.

Everyone wrote down telegram-style:

1. What behaviour in team members hinders me, what behaviour helps me to function effectively?
2. Notes were exchanged.
3. All participants gave a summary of the picture they obtained from the notes and could ask questions to clarify it. Colleagues explained and added to what they had written.

After lunch *Step 3*: conclusions and resolves.

Everyone established for himself what his most important conclusions and resolves were. This was exchanged and sometimes amended by suggestions from others. Agreements were made about the 'follow-up', the primary one being to look through the conclusions together again six months later. Closing.

Preparation. In preparation, contact with the participants well in advance is important. Objectives: becoming acquainted, testing acceptance, problem orientation for the consultant, clarifying ways of working to the participants.

3. Tensions between groups

Various procedures are available for handling problems of some magnitude between departments, groups or levels. Here we will relate two one-day conferences.

3.1 Design of a one-day conference

This is the design of a day devoted to eliminating obstacles to the effective functioning of elements in an organization.

Participants. Representatives of departments in an organization between which relations on the job are tense. This may be the top managers, but it is often possible to allow opinion leaders from their constituencies or even entire sections to participate. The maximum number of participants is around 25.

Objectives.

- specifying the most important obstacles to effective functioning of both groups;
- making agreements for improvement.

Duration. One day with the option to go on the same evening.

Conditions. The participants must want to improve the relations on the job between both groups; they must be willing to work actively on this.

Structure of the day.

(a) Opening and introduction.
(b) The two participating groups meet separately for one hour about:
   - the circumstances and the behaviour of the other group they see as obstacles to their effectiveness;
   - a prediction of the answer the other group will give to this question.
(c) Joint meeting of around 45 minutes about the results of the subgroups. Participants may not enter into discussion; they may ask questions to clarify or give examples until it is clear what is meant by each point and why it is felt to be an obstacle.
(d) The groups talk separately about the results of the general discussion. They ask themselves how '*we*' might be able to reduce the bottlenecks important to the other group. In a brainstorming session, a list of possibilities is made.
(e) In a general session, possibilities are exchanged and clarified; one attempts to reach agreements.

3.2 Confrontation meeting

A variant of this set-up is known as a confrontation meeting. This variant is primarily used in socio-emotional tensions. The procedure discussed under 3.1 is more instrumental in nature.

This intervention was originally described by Blake, Schepard and Mouton (1964). It commences with the images each party has of the other. Such a start is particularly useful if these images are extremely stereotyped and hostile. In that case, the perception the parties have of each other is so far removed from reality that reasonable communication has become well-nigh impossible. After images have been exchanged, they turn to an analysis of the behaviour that led to these images. Who is right is entirely unimportant. The question it revolves around is: 'Where do these images come from?' Once this has been answered, an attempt can be made to discuss suggestions for improving relations.

4. Chairing negotiations

Consultants can expect to be placed in the role of chairman in discussions of a negotiating nature. Understanding the 'logic' of negotiating processes and managing to combine it with the proper procedural proposals are essential.

The following is intended to provide a concrete basis for a chairman. Two types of insights are important:

- the phases in the negotiating process;
- procedural suggestions to increase the chance of success.

These two topics will be elaborated below. This section provides a *complete procedure* for chairing meetings at which participants negotiate. (The procedure can also be used at a more general level as a possible *strategy in change processes with a negotiating nature*.)

In Chapter 5 we described four phases in negotiating:

- preparation;
- initial choice of position;
- search phase;
- impasse and finalization.

These four phases will be defined below for the role of the chairman. Specific procedural suggestions will be given for every phase.

Preparation

Among themselves, parties determine their standpoints and the strategy to be adopted. The chairman is often not involved in these internal deliberations. If he is, he should try to keep parties from committing themselves to one particular solution. Ask about underlying interests and ultimate goals. Try to have them formulate several alternatives.

Initial choice of position

Negotiations generally begin with statements in which the parties present their wishes and interests. Based on facts and on arguments of principle (examples: 'the firm's goals', 'the common interest'), they try to give their position some forcefulness. As chairman, it is important to give them the opportunity to do so without being interrupted by the other participants. Pay particular attention to clarification of underlying goals and interests; sometimes ask questions about them yourself.

Search phase

The parties test each other. How reasonable are their claims? They also probe what interests and ideas play a background role. The consultant is alert to possible combinations of wishes and interests. Parties try to create as much leeway as possible in three ways:

1. In the first place, they try to keep open as many options as possible for themselves: they do not give up anything.
2. They test the tenacity of other parties.
3. They look for possible combinations of interests.

In this phase proposals, sometimes still tentative, are put on the table. These proposals often imply concessions. A chairman can play a very important role here. He can have the parties probe the 'integrative space' by having them present their underlying interests and assumptions. Even more important is that he can prevent endless arguing by focusing the negotiations on concrete proposals. His interventions are intended to urge the participants to exhibit exploring behaviour. A few examples:

- a brainstorming inventory of as many alternative proposals and solutions as possible;
- investigate whether proposals can be integrated by combining claims;
- take a proposal as a basis for further negotiating, avoid discussion of this proposal, ask for suggestions to improve it or for conditions on the basis of which one could agree to it;
- help participants to formulate amendments and conditions if necessary.

One of these points deserves special emphasis. A very fortunate intervention by the chairman is: *use a proposal as a basis for further negotiating!* According to the type of negotiations, this can vary from a draft text of a regulation to the tentative allocation of a budget. *Then focus negotiations on this tentative proposal.* This means restrict arguments and discussion. Ask instead for amendments or conditions which would make the proposal acceptable. This simple behaviour gives a chairman a powerful lever to organize the negotiations more constructively and to speed them up. *Of all the procedural suggestions, this one is the most important!*

Impasse and finalization

By wielding his authority, a chairman can sometimes settle certain points in this phase and thus facilitate a compromise. For sometimes people are not so well equipped to deal with impasses; they tend to rigidify and to make excessive use of pressure. Sometimes time pressure and other 'inconveniences', such as the threat that an unfair regulation will remain in operation, come to his aid in seeking an acceptable compromise.

A good compromise satisfies the following conditions:

- it gives some advantage to parties that have succeeded in linking their claims to generally acknowledged interest and goals;
- it utilizes the integrative possibilities (for instance, a combination of interests in a creative package deal);

- it leaves none of the parties behind in an isolated position or in the role of 'the big loser'.

5. Organizing and structuring the problem approach

These intervention programmes are an elaboration of postulates 5, 6 and 7. They show how, depending on the relational aspect at issue, a confrontation of perspectives and synthesis can be brought about. The other postulates are about the conditions for such a process, primarily about conditioning the power and dependency aspect. The following case is an example of this. But first we want to make an explicit link between the intervention programmes and the view elaborated in Chapter 2 of the four relational aspects characterized by certain tension balances deduced from the central tension balance 'autonomy–mutual dependency'.

Earlier (see e.g. Figure 7.2 and Table 7.1) we indicated that certain behaviour and certain interventions are appropriate to such relational aspect. We described an intervention programme for each aspect. How do these intervention programmes take effect on the relational aspects? What is the specific nature of this effect?

The distinguishing characteristic is that both the autonomy and the interdependency of the parties are profiled and reach a synthesis in an equilibrium. In each programme, we see the profiling take place when the parties work out their own perspectives and present them comprehensively. The consultant makes sure that parties listen actively to each other's perspectives. His most important contribution is keeping opinions, positions and interests moving. He prevents circular discussions and entrenched positions. He pilots parties through a process of exchange and opinion formation. The perspectives of the parties are *facts*. Based on these facts, integration and synthesis take place! This means it is necessary to put parties in a position to present their interests and ideas as co-determinants of a solution. Denying this drives parties to rigid positions and isolation. Integration becomes more and more difficult. *We are confronted by a paradox: in order to integrate better, we must first differentiate well!* Starting from a controlled confrontation, a co-ordinating perspective is developed which links, balances and synthesizes several perspectives.

This process takes a different course per relational aspect. In the *instrumental aspect* there is the balance of tension between the need for consensus and the individual preferences of parties. The consultant organizes the decision-making between parties. He provides procedures to analyse and solve problems. He strives for a mixture of standpoints and views so that all parties get sight of the whole. Once they have this outlook, parties can re-evaluate their own views and make them more realistic. Like this, each individual view is not only a part of the whole, but it affects other views and is influenced and gauged by them. The consultant systematically increased the chance that this actually takes place. His activities form the link between the poles of the operative balance of tension. Schematically:

Consensus ⟨--- Structuring decision-making towards
solution that does justice to preferences ---⟩ Own preference
of parties and is of high quality

Shuttling back and forth between these poles and structuring this process for the parties so that the chance of success increases can be a very important contribution by a consultant.

In the *negotiating aspect* there is the tension between increasing one's own share of the scarce resources and the common interest of increasing the total 'cake' available. Here the consultant tries to achieve workable compromises between parties by structuring the negotiations. Sometimes this goes so far that he winds up in the role of chairman, as shown by the procedure described elsewhere.

Total benefits ⟨--- Structuring the negotiating until
maximum   a workable compromise acceptable ---⟩ Own share
to all parties has been achieved   maximum

Here, too, the consultant tries to regulate the 'traffic' between the two poles in such a way that the chances of workable compromises are increased.

In the *socio-emotional aspect*, it involves promoting the process of mutual understanding. Underlying norms and feelings of identity must be presented in a usable form. The consultant strives for understanding in the parties; 'the best solution' is not the issue, nor is a compromise the objective. It is about achieving workable relations, a relationship that is not undermined by antipathy or strong feelings of resentment and irritation. Schematically:

'We' feeling ⟨--- Structuring and promoting the process
of understanding on both sides until ---⟩ Own identity
mutual understanding has been achieved

One characteristic these processes have in common is their exploratory nature. The first step is as broad a diagnosis of the problem as possible. Movement is essential here. Polarization of positions must be avoided. If the matter has escalated at an earlier stage, discussions must be avoided or very clearly structured. At a more 'normal' level of tension, an inventorying or brainstorming exchange of ideas is an effective technique.

Exploring means stimulating creativity, particularly when problem-solving is on the agenda. Creativity implies movement and flexibility, the pre-eminent characteristics of exploring. Creativity helps in developing alternative solutions, even outside the originally stated frameworks. It facilitates finding creative combinations which integrate several perspectives.

The consulting approach as described in these programmes is also useful in consultancy of longer duration. Exploratory research, alternative solutions, confrontation of reactions, formulation of a tentative solution, working it out with those involved—these are all steps in a consultancy project that can benefit from this approach. This method is indispensable to building up a foothold and achieving acceptance. Sometimes only small groups of insiders are able to recognize the efforts of a consultant as a response to their problems. *There is a tendency for a consultant to postpone the process of confrontation too long.* It sometimes does not really take place until the consultant presents his report. He then tends to regret the ensuing arguing and to find it bothersome. Impasses in the finalization of decision-making, polarization of positions, these are symptoms the consultant tends to regard as cumbersome incidents rather than as an important part of the process. He will have to exhibit inventiveness in dealing with them. He is also handicapped by a tendency on the part of the client to view him as a party with a very pronounced position once he has made his report. This can make it difficult to demonstrate and to encourage explorative behaviour.

In conclusion, the profiling of the three relational aspects advocated here is a very important theme in our thinking on interventions. The reader will recall that a strategy for change for the total organization was described in Chapter 3 in which this profiling was shown to be part of the structure and culture of the organization. We find the same basic idea in this chapter in the consultant's 'handiwork' in dealing with much smaller-scale problems.

6. Case

The following short case description shows something of the confusion and imprecision we sometimes have to face up to in the present state of the art. It shows how an awareness of the various types of relations leads to different interventions and how important 'political' characteristics of a situation can become more conspicuous.

Description

Two departments of a firm came into increasing opposition: an operational department which made use of advanced technical equipment in its work, and a technical department that advised the operational department on the most adequate equipment. Above them was a director. Managers of both departments and the director together made the decisions.

The technical department had recently become more influential. In the past, the operational department could more or less decide what it wanted to have. But increasing technical complexity had given the technical department an opportunity to gain more and more influence. More and more frequently the operational department had to provide all kinds of data, while the technical department decided what was best. This met with fierce resistance from the operational department. Decision-making on these matters started to stagnate. The conflict escalated: avoiding contact, sterotyping, reproaches and accusations, intense personal irritation and such were the order of the day. Employees started lobbying elsewhere in the organization and manœuvring to mobilize support for their plans or for their resistance to the plans of the other party. In other words, the conflict was starting to show all the characteristics of an out of control 'equal vs equal' situation. It also exhibited a few characteristics of a 'high vs low' situation. The party which had become stronger was accused of extreme arrogance, while the other party was found to be rather passive and now and then unreasonably aggressive.

An official of the personnel department enlisted organizational consultants. They felt that intense mutual mistrust lay at the heart of the matter. 'Reduce this first before tackling the instrumental aspect—better procedures of co-ordination and more precise task definitions.' This was their strategy. They decided to use a variant of an intervention known as the confrontation meeting: views were exchanged on behaviour that both sides found to be irritating and frustrating.

It was then investigated how both sides might be able to change this. Several specific problems were extracted from the discussion that deserved priority. Initially, it looked like a few matters had been talked out. The intensity of the conflict was somewhat reduced. Personal relations seemed to improve. Draft solutions to a few problems were advanced. But after a few weeks the improvement turned out not to be genuine. A continuation of the more business-like and problem-oriented approach also had little effect. With a consultant as discussion leader, they tried to solve some of the most important problems. The matter remained deadlocked.

In the meantime other consultants had been called in, initially for another aspect of the problem. They managed to develop an entirely different approach. They set down the most important problems once more on paper, as well as possible solutions. Under their chairmanship the problems were treated point by point in a limited number of talks with the director and the managers of both departments. The consultants formulated *compromises* when they had to. They also had the parties specify their *conditions* on the basis of which they could agree. It was decided in advance that any points on which they could not reach agreement would be decided by a higher echelon after consultation with the director and the consultants. This approach worked. Finally decisions were made, some of them by those involved, others by the higher echelon.

Commentary on the case

Why had the consultants decided on this fairly drastic approach? Closer analysis of the network had made them conclude that in fact there was a power vacuum above the conflicting parties. The director turned out to be incapable of making decisions. This encouraged the parties to continue striving to improve and strengthen their positions and ultimately to a complete power struggle. If a still higher echelon were to intervene, as long as they made sure they had the best cards in their hands, they felt they would come out of it all right at that point.

This development turned out to have a much stronger influence on the behaviour and the relations between parties than the socio-emotional or more instrumental interventions. The last intervention broke this vicious circle, not temporarily, but for good. The consultants succeeded in introducing a few adaptations in the structure which somewhat strengthened the weaker party: better internal organization, improving their ability to take a stand on technical matters. This brought the parties more into balance. In addition, an adjunct director was hired: the effect was a more effective top management which was better capable of emphasizing common interests and of pushing through compromises at a certain point. This was clearly a revision of the network so that fighting behaviour got much less opportunity. The case illustrates the importance of the power and dependency aspect of relations: if one does not succeed in placing problems in this structural framework, one stands a good chance of proposing fairly ineffectual interventions.

This case is a good example of a problem consultants often experience. *In the turbulence of problems and events, it turns out to be difficult to see clearly which central factors can be levers for effective interventions.* The second group of consultants hit the bull's-eye at a certain moment. Seen in retrospect, perhaps it seems logical and self-evident. For a consultant in the middle of things, this was at best one of the options, and it was overshadowed by very urgent matters such as a great deal of mistrust and many very serious bottlenecks in co-ordination, synchronization and task division. *It is in this sort of situation that the theory can prove its usefulness. It can enable one to make out certain patterns more clearly, so that one sees what must be done to find a way out.*

A second problem we encounter in this case is that intervening sometimes places heavy demands on the consultant in terms of his own power and dependency with respect to the positions in the network. The first group of consultants was almost incapable of some interventions because they had no access to the higher echelon. The problems lay precisely at the level of those who had hired them. The second group of consultants had much easier access to the higher echelon and were thus able to fill the power vacuum.

The sometimes fairly powerless position of consultants is partly due to their mutual differences about what adequate interventions really are. Pettigrew (1975) pointed out that disagreement among consultants seriously undermined their power, and that sometimes even elements in the client organization made grateful use of this handicap.

7.6 CONCLUSION

This chapter has described a framework for interventions. Our main concern was a coherent intervention programme, which we have worked out more concretely in the last few sections. In doing this, we pursued the one-on-three model described in this book by indicating how the intervention approach shifts according to the relational aspect that is dominant.

8   In Conclusion

8.1   OBJECTIVE

The *objective* of this book has been to describe an intervention theory which contributes to better solutions to organizational problems and to the development of effective cultural and structural conditions in organizations. The book has expanded upon several important advances in organization theory and has drawn on the practice of consulting. It has attempted to decrease the gap between theory and practice.

This intent is in line with what we have termed the *dynamics* of organizations in our organization theory. The object is to influence them in a positive sense and to get a grip on the vicious circles that can evolve in organizations. In this connection, Elias (1984, p. 48) used a metaphor derived from a story by Edgar Allan Poe, 'The descent into the maelstrom':

A fishing-boat was dragged into a whirlpool. The fishermen were slowly drawn into its bottomless depths. They were sucked downwards along with all kinds of debris along the sides of the ever narrowing vortex. Overcome as they were by vehement emotions and fearing for their very lives, it was utterly impossible for them to see exactly what was going on around them or to think clearly. But one of the fishermen admonished himself and forced himself to observe what was happening. While the other cowered helplessly in the boat, paralysed by the impending disaster, the first one began to see certain regularities and relations in the confusion of events around him. It struck him that smaller objects went down more slowly than large ones. He also rapidly concluded that objects of a cylindrical shape went down more slowly than objects of any other shape. On the basis of this knowledge he could do what was necessary in the situation. He tied himself to a barrel and prepared to jump overboard, signalling his companion to do the same. But the other man remained rigid with fear and clung to the fateful semblance of security of the large fishing boat. The first man jumped overboard and ultimately managed to save himself, while the other perished with boat and all.

This parable figuratively portrays an important thing consultants with a behavioural science background have to offer. In organizations, dynamics can be set in motion which lead to chronic problems. It is often impossible for those caught up in the fray to take enough perspective from the conditions they are in and to make sense of them. We are sometimes in danger of losing sight of the relation between conditioning factors and dynamic processes that can turn into vicious circles, and sometimes a long way from influencing these conditions in a way which can benefit us.

In my view, discerning vicious circles in organizations and putting an end to them should be an important objective of organizational scientists and consultants. Because they are not so much in the midst of things and because of their training and experience, they can recognize such patterns and stop them. This is an important contribution. It can be even more important to influence organizational conditions in such a way that not negative dynamics, but positive dynamic processes are set in motion. Chapter 3, for example, has described how the dynamics can be deflected in the direction of flexibility, internal entrepreneurship and concern for the product.

The added value of consultants lies to an important extent in their recognition of patterns and contexts in the dynamics of organizations. Consulting work sharpens one's acumen for this. The nature of their work gives consultants more opportunities for this than does a manager's job, but more opportunities, too, than have researchers at a university. Managers are at a disadvantage because, in the everyday turbulence and the pressure of the moment, they are seldom in a position to take a perspective and to integrate their experiences systematically with those of others into a coherent whole. Besides, they are shaped by their company's own culture and are dependent on internal 'company politics'. Researchers generally stay too far from practical reality. They busy themselves with building theories that give their more practical counterparts the impression they are aloof armchair philosophers. Or they are so driven by empirical precision that their detailed research results seem trivial and incoherent. Altogether, their findings tend to have such a low practical value that the important test, 'Does it work in practice?', never takes place.

One of the most stimulating sides of the consulting profession is that it obliges consultants to integrate experiences and to create perspectives. Their creativity is constantly challenged. They are market-oriented in this, that is, they focus on the problem areas as they encounter them at clients. The added value of their solutions and interventions lies primarily in the creative combination and integration of the experience they have in this field. In addition to their own experience, they can draw on directly accessible experience from their network of colleagues, from contacts with other consulting firms and active participation in national and international professional organizations. The quality of this network determines to an important extent the quality of the consultant. The best means to further professionalization and a stronger market position is to maintain many forms of intensive exchange in an ever expanding network. This process is given added stimulus when such systematized experience is made available quickly to a wide audience via publications, congresses and management training courses. For this, too, is an interesting market for consultants. The result is that the knowledge becomes readily accessible, and its dissemination rapid. These dynamics, which consultants themselves stimulate, force them to refine even more their arsenal of solutions and interventions, to systematize them further and to pick up new developments even faster.

If a consultant recognizes these dynamics, he can play an active role in them, thus stimulating his own development as well. There are many ways of doing this; examples are:

- ensuring a constant input of a wide range of relevant written information;
- systematically expanding one's own network of personal contacts with a view to relevant experience;
- creating intensive forms of exchange with colleagues (this is perhaps the most powerful one);
- constantly trying to achieve creative combinations of existing insights and skills in one's own repertory of interventions;
- trying out one's own insights by specifying them and by eliciting reactions to them, for example, by submitting papers to congresses or by publishing one's ideas.

Very important, finally, is that a person is well aware of the open and provisional nature of the available knowledge about organizations. Many insights quickly become obsolete. Paradoxically enough, consultants derive a large part of their right to exist from this very fact.

What it boils down to is that every consultant has his own research and development responsibility to live up to, and he must work out an integrative structure for himself in which to place his experiences and insights. The term 'continuing professionalization' covers this activity well, although it may have the ring of an option, of a road one may choose. It is not merely an option, it is an *absolute essential*, at least if a person is to build up and maintain a reasonable market position.

Because of the higher degree of systematization and the higher level of integration of many specific experiences, the knowledge of consultants has an aspect of scientism. It is implicit in the very nature of consulting work, but is limited by it as well. Because the knowledge relates directly to specific problem areas, an integration is lacking. There are but few consultants who concern themselves with, for example, the precise relationships between the fields of quality improvement, product innovation, strategy development, conflict management, effective leadership styles and influencing the culture.

From a commercial point of view, the market behind the demand for integration evidently does not interest consultants. In my view, this is a mistake; because a coherent framework for these fields can only make it easier for managers to influence changes in the desired direction. Highly promising developments have recently been taking place in the field of system-wide change. Precisely these developments have been reflected in this book (Chapter 3). Yet the vast majority of questions put to consultants still relate to small and well-defined areas, and this will not change until exchange and interaction with clients have demonstrated that consultants can also effectively deal with more integrative issues at a 'macro' level.

In fact, universities and especially the business faculties ought to be pioneers in this. But they do not show much sign of it. Perhaps a role is played by the disadvantages seemingly inherent in universities which we cited earlier: armchair theories, incoherent and apparently trivial empirical findings, or a too segmented orientation to limited problem areas. Van Dijk and Punch (1985), both employed at Nijenrode Business University, saw this last drawback as the central factor. They found a remarkable lack of comprehensive and integrative theories in their field, which they considered a serious handicap. They blamed it on the orientation of business schools to solving the practical problems of managers. (In this respect there is a clear correspondence with the work of organizational consultants.) This is rather surprising, for however praiseworthy a practical attitude may be, scientists have a second responsibility. There is, after all, a 'scientific market' where they can take their research results and their integrative theories, where they are less dependent on the commercial aspect of obtaining jobs and projects. Anyway, this is a field of knowledge which is highly dependent on intensive exchange and interaction between theory and practice. Consultants, managers and scientists all have contributions to make. There are plenty of indications that an integration of their insights will prove to be extremely useful in regulating the turbulent and complex flow of events of which we are all part.

8.2 CONFLICT MANAGEMENT AND ORGANIZATIONAL DEVELOPMENT

This book is entitled *Conflict Management and Organization Development*. The integration of these two approaches which we have tried to achieve in this book is based primarily on the following four points:

1. A focus on *relations* between people in organizations. A relational perspective gives adequate attention to interpersonal processes, to *how* these relations work, what sort of behaviour people exhibit and what problems come up in their mutual relations. Briefly, the way in which people get along together gets a great deal of attention. Organizational development has an extremely well-developed eye for this and a good idea of what can be done about it.

2. Another aspect of organizational development we have gladly borrowed is its *arsenal of interventions*. It mainly focuses on socio-emotional and instrumental relations, often against the background of strong interdependencies. The approach described here explicitly accommodates these types of relations and interventions.

3. The *incorporation of power and dependency relations* and *negotiating relations* fills a recognized lacuna in organizational development, not only on the theoretical side but on the side of interventions as well. Organizational development is still fairly biased to socio-emotional and instrumental relational aspects. I do not see why we cannot create just as rich an instrumentation for the other two relational aspects in the long run. This book is intended as a step in this direction.

4. *No matter what type of relation we are talking about, problems in organizations are seen as manifestations of tensions or conflicts between units.* This includes instrumental and socio-emotional relations, because in this book we look at organizations as networks of units between which tensions are by definition present: the tension balance 'autonomy vs dependency' plays a role in all four relational aspects. The implication is that not only relations and relational improvement (organizational development), but also tensions and the management of existing or possible conflicts are central to this approach.

Its incorporation of power phenomena and contrasting interests and its taking into account of more intense forms of conflict make this approach more widely applicable than organizational development. There is another difference in applicability which I would like to discuss briefly. Organizational development aims at system-wide change in the direction of recognized organizational development values such as continuing personal growth, harmonious co-operation, openness and trust. These aims are not stressed in this book. The method explained here is highly problem-oriented, and most of the problems it covers are relatively small scale.* Furthermore, it aims at an integration of several problem areas. In the third place, the intervention theory described here also makes recommendations for large-scale changes but in a way different from organizational development. It does not emphasize the traditional organizational development values. The interventions that we advocate go in a different direction. They are aimed at vitality and competitive power. To achieve this, they use the competitive energy within and between organizations, but at the same time they regulate it. The task of consultants is to help regulate relations between people in a way that decreases the chance of destructive conflicts and wasted energy. A certain tension can be beneficial. Both the organization *and* its employees can profit from it. A certain balance between *both* rivalry *and* co-operation within and between organizations helps keep them competitive. It has been extensively described how the structural and cultural conditions in an organization as a whole can be influenced in a way that increases the chances of a productive tension between units.

---

* This is in my view also the case in the practice of organizational development. Many organizational development interventions are very well suited for all kinds of small-scale problems and are presented thus (French and Bell, 1984; Huse, 1980).

8.3   MOST IMPORTANT POINTS

Seven points should be mentioned as the most important:

1. *The organizational theory used sees power differences and contrasts as normal. This theory makes less socially acceptable behaviour less controversial and more comprehensible. At the same time the theory offers a framework for phenomena of dependence, co-operation and adjustment.*
2. *Power-oriented behaviour and negotiating behaviour are conceptualized in a way that makes them more accessible to interventions.*
3. *Important accomplishments of organizational development are maintained and integrated: an orientation to processes and to the quality of relations between people and groups in organizations, an extensive arsenal of interventions. At the same time some of the weaker sides of organizational development—a too optimistic view of man, not taking into account conflicting interests and power problems and a weak theoretical basis—are remedied somewhat.*
4. *As a theoretical basis, both the systems model and the parties model are too narrow and too one-sided. The network model described here is a 'parties in a system' model. This model is based on the 'mixed nature' of relations. Another important concept of this model is the 'dynamics' of networks. The network model offers room for both systems and parties characteristics of organizations. The link between the two types of characteristics is a central aspect of the network model.*
5. *The recent literature on successful organizations has been incorporated in this book. It has turned out to be possible to integrate a seemingly confusing and contrasting mass of management and organizational principles in the organizational theory described here. This was done by a reducing a motley of recommendations and research results to a limited number of interrelated theoretical elements which also serve as levers for a change strategy.*
6. *This approach contains a systematic procedure for ordering the problems in the relationship between theory and practice, thus putting us in a better position to make the step from theory to practice and vice versa.*
7. *A comprehensive change strategy is presented, a strategy which provides concrete guide-lines for effectively influencing the structural and cultural conditions in organizations. The strategy provides levers to develop motivation and flexibility. It specifies how we can achieve an organizational culture of internal entrepreneurship.*

8.4   FINAL REMARK

It was my intention to describe an intervention theory which is not only related to some established theories on organizations and on interventions, but which is also closely attuned to concrete problems and practical interventions—closely enough, I hope, so that it is relatively easy to recognize and can serve as a guide-line for thinking and acting. A continual confrontation with intervention experiences can act as a test of the intervention theory described here, and will serve as the basis for its improvement. Intervening, comparing our experiences to those of others, discussing them, forming opinions, trying out alterations, more discussion—in short, a sort of trial-and-error process will have to develop this intervention theory further. For an intervention theory is something that must be socially accepted and made more useful and applicable by people who have to deal with organizational problems and who now and then take time to think about them systematically.

8.5 SUMMARY OF THE BOOK

Organizations are networks. The increasing complexity of organizations can corrode their vitality. Relations between organizational units are character-ized by impulses towards mutual dependency *and* towards autonomy. We see this tension balance in its clearest form in the division of authorities and responsibilities, but also in work processes, socio-emotional ties and negotiat-ing processes. The tension balances in these four types of interdependencies are expressed in the structure of the organization and in the way in which people deal with it: the organizational culture. It is important to know how and in what direction structure and culture can be developed if we want to improve the functioning of people in organizations and to increase the vitality of organiz-ations. That has been the subject of this book; at the same time, it has pre-sented an arsenal of interventions, skills and solutions for the inevitable tensions and conflicts between the units of an organization.

Formulated still more concisely: the survival power of organizations depends on the ability of their employees to deal with the ever expanding and denser networks of internal and external interdependencies. This is condi-tional on a reduction of complexity and on debureaucratization. At an operational level it demands greater skill in dealing with many sorts of interdependencies, including the tensions and frictions inherent in them.

9 Update: Organizational Conditions for Competitive Advantage

BRIDGING THE GAP BETWEEN THEORY AND PRACTICE

This update builds upon the concepts elaborated in this book. It provides diagnostic tools and recent findings of relevance for our organizational model. We have added this chapter to this edition because it summarizes our recent experiences and ideas based on the application of the concepts in this book.

9.1 INTRODUCTION

What are the levers for successful organization design? What conditions determine competitive power? What design makes for motivation and commitment?

A wide array of recommendations is available: team development, cultural change, leadership skills, inspiring mission statement, less hierarchy, decentralization, better information systems, intrapreneurship, improved communication, small autonomous units, informal style, customer orientation, building on core competencies. But such a laundry list does not provide much of a solution.

9.2 DEVELOPING BETTER CONCEPTS AND MODELS

In Chapters 2 and 3 we have described an integrative concept. Briefly summarized, this is the concept of organizations as networks of units balancing autonomy and interdependency. Particular patterns of autonomy and interdependency show a strong competitive power. A general characteristic of these patterns is the articulation of autonomy as well as interdependency among units.

Practice-oriented authors, trying to find some integrative vehicle, often come up with organization models ordered around a few basic categories. The categories used most frequently are strategy, structure, culture and information systems (Figure 9.1). Some authors add categories such as technology, human resources and leadership. One of the best-known models of this kind is the 7S model introduced by Peters and Waterman (1982).

These models provide for a neat clustering of important factors. They are much used by managers and consultants. At the same time they show some serious limitations. One problem is of an analytical nature. The various elements are difficult to separate. A way of working, does that come under culture, structure or strategy? If it is defined in terms of delineation of tasks and procedures, we call it structure. But if it is not formalized in this manner, does that mean it is culture? If it is proclaimed by the top, do we call it strategy?

An even more important problem concerns the way in which the separate elements are linked. Authors design boxes with arrows and connecting lines. What do these arrows and lines stand for? This remains obscure. Specific relationships and influences are suggested. The 'what' and 'how' remain implicit.

This problem is all the more urgent because the everyday practice of organizations often entails a multitude of changes: not only developing a clearer strategy but also structural adjustments, information projects, changes in management style and quality actions. How can we make all this into a coherent whole? How do we ensure that the separate changes fit into an

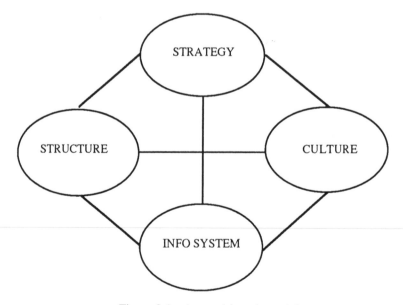

Figure 9.1   A practitioner's model

integrative framework? How do we gain such a clear understanding of their relationship that we can make sure they complement and reinforce each other, and that we do not steer them as separate processes? The models in question are too shallow to accomplish this.

Despite these disadvantages and despite their low academic reputation, these models are used frequently. Apparently they have much more to offer to practitioners than the more sophisticated, scientific models that are available. One of the advantages they offer is a simple and elegant way to arrange important issues and processes. This classification may be primitive, more like a checklist of categories. And it may also be rather crude: categories overlap, and there may be a lack of understanding the relations between categories and more basic processes. Nevertheless, it is a classification, and it provides an overview in understandable terms. So, for instance, the conditions discussed earlier in Chapters 2 and 3 fit in the model as shown in Figure 9.2.

However, if we are concerned with the way in which strategy, structure, culture and information systems influence each other, this classification does not help us much. And that confronts us with the problem of the nature of organizations and the best way to express it.

If we wish to understand how organizations function, we should focus on human behaviour, attitudes and the problems and solutions as people experience them. Organizations are networks of people; they are arrangements of communication, perception, meaning and behaviour between people. Organizational theory provides a multitude of ways to capture these arrangements in models and concepts. We think the concept of interdependencies provides

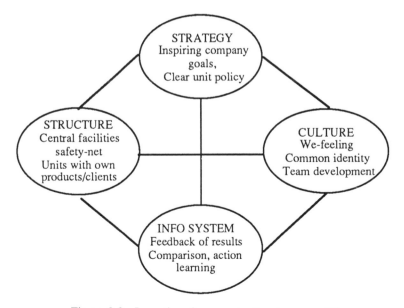

Figure 9.2   Incentives for organizational success (1)

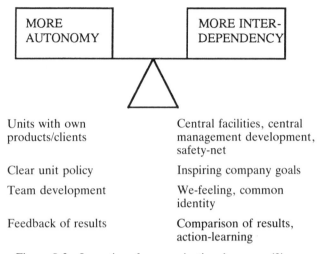

MORE AUTONOMY	MORE INTER-DEPENDENCY
Units with own products/clients	Central facilities, central management development, safety-net
Clear unit policy	Inspiring company goals
Team development	We-feeling, common identity
Feedback of results	Comparison of results, action-learning

Figure 9.3   Incentives for organizational success (2)

the most promising possibilities. Structure and culture are both characteristics of interdependencies; structure in a formalized way, culture more in terms of attitudes and perceptions. Strategy and information systems also give shape to interdependencies. For us, organizational design is arranging interdependencies in such a way that both the autonomy and the interdependency of units are reinforced in a sound balance. In this way an understanding of the relation between separate changes becomes possible. From this concept, a reordering of the incentives for organizational success (as described in Figure 9.2) leads to the classification as expressed in Figure 9.3.

This reshuffling shows more clearly how things fit together. The separate elements under the headings strategy, structure, culture and information system can be ordered in a more meaningful way on the basis of their impact on the autonomy–interdependency balance. It is more meaningful because this makes it easier to show how elements can be designed in a coherent and mutually reinforcing way. More meaningful also because of the more direct relationship with the crucial issues of less complexity and higher motivational levels in organizations.

9.3   ORGANIZATIONAL THEORY LAGS BEHIND PRACTICE

For organizations to survive, they must effectively manage the expanding and densifying networks of internal and external interdependencies. Less complexity and debureaucratization are necessary conditions. Companies can get into difficulties through internal rigidity, lack of innovation and demotivated workers; thus it is necessary to restructure complicated dependency relations and to work towards flexible units that are linked directly to the market. If we manage to combine this with strong incentives towards

mutual exchange and support, we contribute to more competitive organizations. Practice does not wait for solid theory and concepts to guide this
development. By trial and error, managers organize their companies as
effectively as possible, sometimes by following successful competitors. Often
this is a blind process which managers try to steer intuitively. In our opinion it
can be managed more consciously by aiming at certain configurations of
autonomy and interdependency which by now have proved to be successful.
These highly competitive configurations are showing up in individual companies as well as between companies; for instance, conglomerates may
sometimes be dissolved by a form of management buy-out while units retain a
few vital links and interdependencies with other concern units. The Rank
Xerox network experiment is an original example of another pattern. Carefully selected and well-trained employees are helped to leave the organization; they then set up a company on their own while continuing to offer their
services to the parent company. The activities of their new companies are
often quite similar to the previous jobs of the ex-employees. The object is to
limit the overhead while committing valuable people to the organization
(Judkins and West, 1986).

This is an example of a development from 'large' to 'small-in-large'. There
is also a movement from 'small' to 'small-in-large' which is manifested in
alliances through franchising formulas, in purchase or sales combinations or
under umbrella concerns, where top management's involvement is limited to
a few crucial interchanges and interdependencies. Interesting forms of
umbrella concerns are described in a recent article in *Fortune* (21 December
1987), Goodbye Corporate Staff. The article terms such companies the 'new
minimalist corporations'. They are remarkable for their high competitive
energy and their typical combination of centralization with decentralization.
The 'hollow company' and the 'virtual corporation' are other manifestations
of this type of configuration (*Business Week*, 8 February 1993).

Developing interdependencies between organizations in carefully selected
areas strengthens their competitive power. This is also true of the largest
companies. Large multinationals, which are outspoken competitors (such as
Philips and Sony), co-operate to set standards in guiding their research and
development. In our view, the rapidly increasing interest in 'strategic
alliances' is another symptom of the same development (Bleeke and Ernst,
1993). There are entrepreneurs who find their strength primarily in organizing
alliances. They do not produce anything, their role is that of middleman.
Take for example the following situation: an ice hockey helmet is designed in
Scandinavia, made ready for production and tuned to the demands of the
global market in the United States, it is produced in Korea and distributed
from Japan. Miles (1989) presents a series of examples of such network
organizations in the fashion business, the film industry and publishing companies. In itself, such a network organization is not new. The new element is
the diffusion of this model to an increasing number of market sectors. Being
the intermediary in such a network organization is not necessarily an indepen-

dent function. Any of the participants can act as intermediary. It is, however, the crucial function. Companies who take on this function are sometimes given the derogatory name 'hollow company'. In our opinion it is more appropriate to regard this as a high-quality form of entrepreneurship. In this way we find a modern and catching variation of Schumpeter's 'old-fashioned' definition of entrepreneurship as 'neue Kombinationen machen' (Schumpeter, 1954).

Another pattern can be seen in thriving configurations such as the world trade centres in Amsterdam and Rotterdam and in the Schiphol airport area, which boom despite an oversupply of office space and industrial estates in The Netherlands. In these configurations, real estate agents no longer deal in property as such: they deal in interdependencies. The trade is in entrances to world-embracing interdependency chains which offer optimal opportunities for creating new combinations.

We described an integrative concept applicable to these developments. 'Integrative', because it brings together contrasting movements in organizations. We tried to incorporate the dual nature of organizations by using the autonomy–interdependency concept. This concept accommodates the dilemmas, paradoxes and built-in tensions in organizations. These tensions are a source of energy; they can also have destructive effects. When properly directed and balanced they work out positively and generate motivation and vitality.* The struggle with this duality is both theoretical and practical. Often theory lags behind actual practice. Miles and Snow (1986) state that organizations are emerging for which we have to develop new integrative concepts. This search for concepts which integrate various perspectives cannot be seen as distinct from the increasing number of organizations which derive their vitality from combinations of apparently contrasting organizational principles: central and decentral, loose and tight, differentiation and integration.

9.4   THE EMERGING MODEL OF ORGANIZATIONS

The model of the organization as a functional pyramid or as a divisionalized structure is no longer suited for the modern type of organization; rather, it is a

---

* This duality can also be seen in the differentiation–integration perspective of Lawrence and Lorsch (1967). They described several ways to articulate and to balance these two forces. It is interesting to see how recent developments add to our possibilities to direct and balance these forces. Lawrence and Lorsch elaborate as integrative mechanisms: hierarchy, informal contacts, formal co-ordination, specialized integrators and conflict regulation skills. Compare these for instance with the five co-ordinating mechanisms on which Mintzberg (1979) bases his typology, or with the incentives to strengthen the interdependencies between and within the units of an organization as discussed in this chapter. As far as differentiation is concerned Lawrence and Lorsch concentrate on functional differentiation. The more recent approach is stressing the importance of organizing around units with products and/or markets of their own. These units are functionally relatively integrated.

network of units that are free to act while retaining their links to one another. *Units are autonomous, while cultivating simultaneously those interdependencies that give them a competitive edge.* In addition, organizations rely on more horizontal market-like co-ordination mechanisms, one of the most important of which is the continuous feedback of results. This gives a different substance to the relationship of centralized to decentralized. The swing of the pendulum from central to decentral becomes a dynamic tension balance of *both* central *and* decentral. The direction in which the network moves and the quality of relations within it are shaped by the more central units, but the units also show responsibility for this. The horizontal exchange and co-ordination in particular, demand that every unit be an active network member. This theme is repeated within units: teams are effective only if they know they are responsible for the organizational unit; individuals can be prominent only if they feel a responsibility for the team of which they are a part.

These processes demand certain social skills of the participants: initiative and an eagerness to show results, combined with the activation of flexible horizontal relations in which integrative potential is developed and new combinations can be formed. The ability to negotiate constructively and creatively and to function well in teams is indispensable for this.

In its most advanced form, we see the 'both/and' nature of relations in such a horizontal network expressed at each intersection. There is a feeling of responsibility for the unit as well as for the larger whole of which it is a part. Each unit focuses on improving its own results, but it is also a microcosm of the totality and can help compensate where capacities are lacking. Figure 9.4 shows some characteristics of this design. Mostly by trial and error, this type of organization is becoming a reality. The theme has countless variations, but the basic pattern is returning. For example, consider the following two entirely different organizations, both of which have developed in this direction:

- The BSO (a software development firm in The Netherlands) design is based on the principle of cell division. Units have a limit of 65 employees; if they grow beyond that number, they are split up. The units are independent companies with responsibility for their sales, recruitment, personnel policy, purchasing and investments: only financial systems and part of research and development are centralized staff services. This firm is one of the fastest growing software houses in The Netherlands.
- Some co-operatives in The Netherlands have traditionally followed a pattern that is increasingly evolving in the direction described. For example, the Holland Flower Auction consists of 3000 autonomous entrepreneurs; these entrepreneurs have considerably strengthened their position through their concerted efforts on the client market. Furthermore, the Holland Flower Auction is in a position to mobilize all kinds of forms of expertise and information to which completely autonomous companies would have less direct access. This type of configuration has proven to be a great

Central:
- Specification of the strategy (an inspiring statement of the core business and common values).
- Development of the organization in the direction of units that are responsible for their performance.
- Stimulation and facilitation of units to make their own results visible and to work systematically on improving performance.
- Attention to the quality of communication, for example by ensuring a good horizontal exchange of results and ideas to improve performance.
- Selection and strengthening of critical interdependencies, for example core competencies, management development, financial systems or economies of scale.

Decentral:
- Units formulate their own output indicators within the policy framework.
- Units set up their own plans to improve results.
- There is a high degree of unit autonomy to determine what means will be employed in what ways to achieve better results.
- Units are free to profile themselves according to their own style and identity.
- Units have sufficient resources to achieve their own plans; there is little dependency on central departments.
- Supporting services are farmed out; there is a market relationship with the remaining central services.

Figure 9.4   Emerging balances: central and decentral

competitive power on the world market. The co-operative flower auctions in The Netherlands handle 60 per cent of the world trade in flowers.

Examples of other variants were given earlier in this chapter. Johnston and Lawrence (1988) also give a diversity of examples; they have observed that links in the production chain are becoming more autonomous and are connected by horizontal—rather than vertical—co-ordination mechanisms. Part of the textile industry in Italy, the large automobile manufacturers in Japan, some large publishing companies and film makers in the United States, in their most competitive forms, these companies take the autonomy of units to an extreme, while still retaining and perfecting carefully selected interdependencies. Bahrami and Evans (1989) provide more supplementary evidence of this development. Their 'bi-modal form' comes pretty close to the dual nature of organizational relations as described here. An important characteristic is the simultaneousness of centralized and decentralized. They describe this organizational configuration as emerging in the high technology firms they researched. The study of Feldman (1989) confirms the same pattern.

This type of organization is on the rise because it can better deal with competition. The most important reasons for this are less bureaucracy and the mobilization of a high energy level. *We are going through a transition to a higher integration level, one that is equipped for more complexity!*

9.5 CONCLUSIONS

Organizations are networks. Relations between units are characterized by impulses towards mutual dependency and towards autonomy. Structure, strategy, culture and information systems offer levers to generate a positive dynamic of increasing motivation and vitality. This can be done by a balanced articulation of the autonomy as well as the interdependency of units. Some incentives to achieve this are presented for instance in Table 3.1 (p. 41).

Our knowledge concerning important aspects of organizations can be translated in its effects on the autonomy–interdependency balance. Strategy, structure, culture and information systems are means to influence this balance.

We feel the autonomy–interdependency concept offers two major advantages for matters of organizational design:

1. It clarifies the connection between the separate areas because we have a common denominator for the multitude of interventions and changes. We are therefore better able to judge whether we are acting consistently, and to what extent changes reinforce each other.
2. The interventions and changes in these areas are immediately tested for their effect on the autonomy–interdependency tension balance. As we argued above, this effect is of crucial importance for the flexibility and market orientation of units and for the motivation of employees.

DIAGNOSIS FOR CHANGE

We will present two diagnostic instruments. The instruments provide a link between the concepts and the change process. In our opinion, sound concepts should provide, in a direct way, levers for organizational change. The instruments specify these levers and provide the nuts and bolts to initiate and steer the process.

Each tool is preceded by an introduction which very briefly describes the underlying concepts.

The instrument 'conditions for motivation' is intended for management teams searching for clues to improve their organization. It builds directly on our model of organizational design (see Chapters 2, 3 and 9).

The second instrument 'stimulating conditions for the improvement of results' builds on the same concept. It has been used in teams of managers, who each supervise a department. It is a useful intervention for teams engaged in projects of continuous improvement or total quality.

DIAGNOSTIC INSTRUMENT: 'CONDITIONS FOR MOTIVATION'

Introduction

Greater quality, more service, more flexibility, cost awareness, innovative capacity become the battle cries. Programmes and instruments are made available to promote all this. Programmes and instruments can offer real help but it soon becomes clear that commitment and motivation are critical factors.

Motivation cannot be developed by a quick fix. It is related to organizational conditions. We refer to conditions and incentives in terms of strategy, structure, culture and information. The questionnaire below describes 28 possibilities. It enables management teams to make up their minds about the most promising leverage points. It can also be used to learn how units in the organization experience their situation and what suggestions they have in mind.

The instrument

This instrument has been designed to indicate how your organization is balancing autonomy and interdependency. This balance is a key factor determining the motivation and commitment of individual organizational members. It is also directly related to the common purpose and identity of the organization as a whole.

The instrument provides clues about the opportunities in your organization to raise motivation. The questions refer to your work situation, and have been designed to elicit your opinions. There is therefore no such thing as a 'right or 'wrong' answer.

Your responses will be treated confidentially. Please answer the questions as frankly as possible. You are requested to respond to each question twice; first for the *current* situation and then for the *desired* situation.

Questionnaire

		To a very slight degree	← Reasonable, fair →			To a very high degree
1	Improvements and renewal are stimulated in our department.					
	NOW	1	2	3	4	5
	DESIRED	1	2	3	4	5
2	We have clearly defined areas of responsibility in our department (own clients/products/markets).					
	NOW	1	2	3	4	5
	DESIRED	1	2	3	4	5

Questionnaire (*cont.*)

		To a very slight degree	← Reasonable, fair →			To a very high degree
3	I know how our customers regard the products and/or services of our department.					
	NOW	1	2	3	4	5
	DESIRED	1	2	3	4	5
4	I am aware of the costs of the different products/services of our department.					
	NOW	1	2	3	4	5
	DESIRED	1	2	3	4	5
5	Departments in our organization have highly motivating objectives.					
	NOW	1	2	3	4	5
	DESIRED	1	2	3	4	5
6	When an important job vacancy occurs a suitable candidate is sought within our own organization.					
	NOW	1	2	3	4	5
	DESIRED	1	2	3	4	5
7	This organization stimulates horizontal job rotation.					
	NOW	1	2	3	4	5
	DESIRED	1	2	3	4	5
8	Our department has its own budget.					
	NOW	1	2	3	4	5
	DESIRED	1	2	3	4	5
9	There is a strong relationship between rewards and achievement in this organization.					
	NOW	1	2	3	4	5
	DESIRED	1	2	3	4	5
10	When our department is 'up against it' it can count on support from the rest of the organization.					
	NOW	1	2	3	4	5
	DESIRED	1	2	3	4	5
11	Ideas and initiatives from our department are taken seriously in the rest of the organization.					
	NOW	1	2	3	4	5
	DESIRED	1	2	3	4	5

Questionnaire (*cont.*)

		To a very slight degree	← Reasonable, fair →			To a very high degree
12	Communication between our department and higher organizational levels and central departments is good.					
	NOW	1	2	3	4	5
	DESIRED	1	2	3	4	5
13	People in our department feel personally responsible for the results of their work.					
	NOW	1	2	3	4	5
	DESIRED	1	2	3	4	5
14	Departments in our organization learn from each other's experiences.					
	NOW	1	2	3	4	5
	DESIRED	1	2	3	4	5
15	The results of our department are made visible to us from time to time.					
	NOW	1	2	3	4	5
	DESIRED	1	2	3	4	5
16	We have the information to compare the results of our department with those of other departments.					
	NOW	1	2	3	4	5
	DESIRED	1	2	3	4	5
17	Everyone who works here knows what the organization as a whole stands for.					
	NOW	1	2	3	4	5
	DESIRED	1	2	3	4	5
18	Senior management of this organization checks our views before determining important matters of policy.					
	NOW	1	2	3	4	5
	DESIRED	1	2	3	4	5
19	My supervisor is interested in my ideas.					
	NOW	1	2	3	4	5
	DESIRED	1	2	3	4	5
20	This organization has inspiring objectives.					
	NOW	1	2	3	4	5
	DESIRED	1	2	3	4	5

Questionnaire (*cont.*)

	To a very slight degree	← Reasonable, fair →		To a very high degree
21 I get stimulating suggestions about my work from my colleagues in my department.				
NOW	1	2	3	4	5
DESIRED	1	2	3	4	5
23 Our entire organization is focused on 'doing it better' than other similar organizations.				
NOW	1	2	3	4	5
DESIRED	1	2	3	4	5
24 There is an informal, co-operative climate in our department.				
NOW	1	2	3	4	5
DESIRED	1	2	3	4	5
25 The different departments within this organization co-operate effectively.				
NOW	1	2	3	4	5
DESIRED	1	2	3	4	5
26 Senior management is aware of the problems experienced within the organization.				
NOW	1	2	3	4	5
DESIRED	1	2	3	4	5
27 I personally subscribe to our department's policies and objectives.				
NOW	1	2	3	4	5
DESIRED	1	2	3	4	5
28 This organization does a great deal for its members.				
NOW	1	2	3	4	5
DESIRED	1	2	3	4	5

Now that you have completed the questionnaire, do you have any additional remarks or comments? You may write these down in the space below.

Many thanks for your co-operation!

Scoring form

Please enter your responses in the following table.

Autonomy   **Interdependency**

Question	Now	Desired	Absolute difference	Question	Now	Desired	Absolute difference
1				6			
2				7			
3				10			
4				11			
5				12			
8				14			
9				17			
13				18			
15				20			
16				22			
19				23			
21				25			
24				26			
27				28			
Totals							

Subsequently, you may enter your totals on the profile sheet.

The higher you scored on autonomy and interdependency, the greater the chance that high levels of dedication and motivation are characteristic of your department and your organization.

Scoring profiles

AUTONOMY		INTERDEPENDENCY	
now	desired	now	desired

70	-				- 70
60	-				- 60
50	-				- 50
40	-				- 40
30	-				- 30
20	-				- 20
10	-				- 10

Leverage points for change

With regard to which questions is the difference between current and desired situations the greatest?

Do you see any opportunities to do something about it?
If so, formulate a few concrete action steps.

. . . .

. . . .

DIAGNOSTIC INSTRUMENT: 'STIMULATING CONDITIONS FOR THE IMPROVEMENT OF RESULTS'

Introduction

The notion behind the following eight questions is that the art is to enhance both the sense of responsibility for 'own department' and the strength of the whole. Does the idea of 'own shop' and 'doing it together' appeal to you? This form will enable you to determine your organization's position in this respect.

Please indicate the degree to which the following statements apply to your organization.

Questionnaire

	To a very slight degree	← Reasonable, fair →			To a very high degree

'OWN SHOP'

1   The departments clearly have their own areas of responsibility; their own customers/own products.

NOW	1	2	3	4	5
DESIRED	1	2	3	4	5

2   The people in the departments know how the customers regard their own products/services.

NOW	1	2	3	4	5
DESIRED	1	2	3	4	5

3   The climate within the department stimulates the employees to do things better.

NOW	1	2	3	4	5
DESIRED	1	2	3	4	5

4   The results of the departments are made visible on a regular basis.

NOW	1	2	3	4	5
DESIRED	1	2	3	4	5

'TOGETHER'

1   Communication with higher echelons and with the central departments is all right.

NOW	1	2	3	4	5
DESIRED	1	2	3	4	5

2   Ideas and initiatives from departments are given every opportunity in this organization.

NOW	1	2	3	4	5
DESIRED	1	2	3	4	5

3   The departments in this organization learn from one another's experiences.

NOW	1	2	3	4	5
DESIRED	1	2	3	4	5

Questionnaire (*cont.*)

	To a very slight degree	← Reasonable, fair →			To a very high degree
4 Everybody who works here knows what the organization as a whole stands for.					
NOW	1	2	3	4	5
DESIRED	1	2	3	4	5

What factors deserve priority in your opinion?

. . . .

. . . .

Bibliography

Argyris, C. (1970) *Intervention theory and method*. Reading, Mass., Addison-Wesley.
Argyris, C. (1972) *The applicability of organizational sociology*. Cambridge, University Press.
Argyris, C. (1974) *Management en organisatie-ontwikkeling*. Alphen aan den Rijn, Samsom.
Aubert, V. (1971) Belangen-en waarden conflicten, twee manieren van conflictoplossing. In: Peper, B. and Schuyt, K. (eds.), *Proeven van rechtssociologie uit het werk van Vilhelm Aubert*. Universitaire Pers.

Bach, G. R., Wijden, P. (1969) *The intimate enemy*. New York, Morrow.
Bahrami, H., Evans, S. (1989) Emerging organizational regimes in high technology firms: the bi-modal form. *Human Resource Management*, 25–50.
Baldridge, J. V. (1971) *Power and conflict in the university*. New York, Wiley.
Beckhard, R. (1969) *Organization development: strategies and models*. Reading, Mass., Addison-Wesley.
Beekman, W. *et al.* (1979) De bruikbaarheid van een contingentie-model en een machtsspelmodel in een organisatieadviesproject. *M & O, Tijdschrift voor organisatiekunde en sociaal beleid*, 358–79.
Blake, R. R., Mouton, J. S. (1961) Reactions to intergroup competition under win–lose conditions. *Management Science*, 420–35.
Blake, R. R., Mouton, J. S. (1969) *Building a dynamic corporation through grid organizational development*. Reading, Addison-Wesley.
Blake, R. R., Mouton, J. S. and Sloma, R. L. (1965) The union–management intergroup laboratory: strategy of resolving intergroup conflict. *Journal of Applied Behavioural Science*. 25–58.
Blake, R. R., Schepard, H. A., Mouton, J. S. (1964) *Managing intergroup conflict in industry*. Houston, Gulf Publ. Co.
Blau, P. M. (1962) Patterns of choice in interpersonal relations. *American Sociological Review*, 41–55.
Bleeke, J., Ernst, D. (ed.) (1993) *Collaborating to compete*. Chichester, Wiley.
Boekestijn, C., De psychologie vna relaties tussen groepen. In: Jaspers, J. M. F., Vlist, R. van der (eds.), *Sociale psychologie in Nederland: De kleine groep*. Deventer, Van Loghum Slaterus.
Bos, A. H. (1974) *Oordeelsvorming in groepen*. Wageningen, Veenman.
Bowers, D. G. (1973) OD techniques and their results in 23 organizations: The Michigan ICL study. *Journal of Applied Behavioral Science*, 21–43.
Bradford, L. P. (1974) *National training laboratories, its history 1947–1970*. Bethel, NTL.
Bradford, L. P., Gibb, J. R., Benne, K. D. (eds.) (1964) *T-group theory and laboratory method: Innovation in re-education*. New York, Wiley.
Breedveld, T. (1980) Interdependentie als factor bij samenwerking tussen organisaties. In: Greve, W. B. de, Vrakking, W. J. (eds.), *Strategie van samenwerking tussen organisaties in welzijns-en gezondheidswerk*. Lochem, De Tijdstroom.

Bunt, P. A. E. van de (1978) *De organisatieadviseur: begeleider of expert*. Alphen aan den Rijn, Samsom.
Bunt, P. A. E. van de, Haaften, K. L. van (1981) *De voordelen van interim management als agogische techniek*. Interne publikatie vakgroep sociale psychologie. Free University, Amsterdam.
Butler, R. J., Astley, W. G., Hickson, D. J., Mollory, G. Wilson, D. (1979) Strategic decision making in organizations: concepts of content and process. *International Studies of Management and Organization*. 5-36.

Chesler, M., Lohmann, J. (1971) Changing schools through student advocacy. In: Schmuck, R. A., Miles, R. B., *Organization development in schools*. Palo Alto.
Chin, R., Benne, K. D. (1969) General strategies for effecting changes in human systems. In: Bennis, W. G. *et al.* (eds.), *The planning of change*. New York, Rinehart & Winston.
COP SER (1979) *Middenkader onder druk*. Assen, van Gorcum.
Corwin, R. G. (1969) Patterns of organizational conflict. *Administrative Science Quarterly*. 507-20.
Coser, L. (1964) *The functions of social conflict*. Glencoe, Ill., Free Press.
Cozijnsen, A. J., Ezerman, G. C. (1984) *Topmanagers over management, afl. 1: Bestuurders op weg naar herstel*. Kluwer, Deventer.
Crozier, M. (1964) *The bureaucratic phenomenon*. Chicago, University of Chicago Press.
Cyert, P. M., Dill, W. R., March, J. G. (1958) The role of expectations in business decision-making. *Administrative Science Quarterly*. 307-40.

Dalton, M. (1954) The role of supervision. In: Kornhauser, A., Dubin, R., Ross, A. (eds.), *Industrial conflict*. New York, McGraw-Hill.
Dalton, M. (1959) *Men who manage*. New York, Wiley.
Deal, T. E., Kennedy, A. A. (1982) *Corporate cultures*. Addison-Wesley, Reading.
Deutsch, M. (1973) *The resolution of conflict*. New Haven, Yale University Press.
Drucker, P. F. (1963) *Managing for results*. London.
Dubin, R. (1959) Stability of human organization. In: Haire, M. (ed.), *Modern organizational theory*. New York, Wiley.
Dupont, C. (1982) *La negotiation: conduite, theorie, application*. Daloz.
Dutton, J. M., Walton, R. E. (1966) Interdepartmental conflict and cooperation: two contrasting studies. *Human Organization*. 207-20.
Dijck, J. J. J. (1977) Het spanningsveld van individu en organisatie: een sociologische optiek. In: Cornelis, P. A., (eds.), *Het spanningsveld tussen individu en organisatie*. Deventer, Kluwer.
Dijck, J. J. J. (1980) De gedesoriënteerde organisatie-adviseur naar een nieuwe stijl van denken en handelen. In: Bunt, P. A. E. van de, Lammers C. J. (eds.), *Organisatie verandering en organisatieadvieswerk*. Alphen aan den Rijn, Samsom.
Dijk, N. M. H. van, Punch, M. E. (1985) *Het dilemma van de bedrijfskunde, Intermediar*.
Dijk, P. van, Kamp, J., Rensen, R. (1985) *De stijl van de leider*. Bert Bakker, Amsterdam.

Elias, N. (1969) *Die Höfische Gesellschaft*. Berlin, Luchterhand. In English (1983): *The court society*. Oxford Basil Blackwell; New York, Pantheon.
Elias, N. (1970) *Sociologie en geschiedenis*. Amsterdam, Van Gennep.
Elias, N. (1971) *Wat is sociologie?* Utrecht, Spectrum. In English (1978): *What is Sociology?* London, Hutchinson.
Elias, N., Scotson, J. L. (1977) *De gevestigden en de buitenstaanders*. Utrecht Spectrum. (In English (1965): *The established and the outsiders*. London, Frank Cass & Co).

Elias, N. (1984) *De eenzaamheid van stervenden in onze tijd.* Amsterdam, Meulenhof. In English (1985): *The loneliness of the dying.* Oxford, Basil Blackwell.

Emerson, R. E. (1962) Power-dependence relations. *American Sociological Review,* 31–41.

Etzioni, A. (1964) *Modern organizations.* Englewood Cliffs, New Jersey, Prentice-Hall.

Ezerman, G. C. (1977) Dilemma's van een externe organisatie-adviseur. *Tijdschrift voor agologie,* 148–62.

Ezerman, G. C., Delden, P. J. van (1978) De smalle marges van het organisatie-advieswerk: een casebeschrijving. In: Huyg, J. P. *et al.* (eds.), *Leren en leven met groepen.* Alphen aan den Rijn, Samsom.

Feldman, S. P. (1989) The broken wheel: the inseparability of autonomy and control in innovation within organizations. *Journal of Management Studies,* 2.

Filley, A. C. (1975) *Interpersonal conflict resolution.* Illinois, Glenview, Scott, Foresman.

Fink, C. F. (1968) Some conceptual difficulties in the theory of social conflict. *Journal of Conflict Resolution,* 412–66.

Fisher, R., Ury W., (1981) *Getting to yes.* Boston, Houghton Mifflin.

French, W. L., Bell, C. H. (1984) *Organization development.* Englewood Cliffs, Prentice-Hall.

Friedlander, F., Brown, R. D. (1974) Organization development. *Annual Review of Psychology,* 313–41.

Frost, P. J. *et al.* (1985) *Organizational culture.* Sage, London.

Gardner, B. B., Moore, D. (1955) *Human relations in industry.* Homewood, Ill., Irwin.

Gardner, B. B., Whyte, W. F. (1945) The man in the middle: positions and problems of the foreman. *Applied Anthropology.*

Gils, M. R. van (1977) Macht in perspectief. In: Bunt, A. W. J. E. van de, Halbertsma, K. T. A., Mulder, M. (eds.), *Macht in en rond organisaties.* Alphen aan den Rijn, Samsom.

Gils, M. R. van (1978) De organisatie van organisaties: aspecten van interorganisationele samenwerking. *M & O, Tijdschrift voor organisatiekunde en sociaal beleid,* 9–31.

Glasl, F. (1980) *Konflikt management.* Bern/Stuttgart, Hauptverlag.

Glasl, F., Houssaye, J. de la (1972) *Organisatie ontwikkeling in de praktijk.* Amsterdam, Agon Elsevier.

Goodstein, L. D., Boyer, R. K. (1972) Crisis intervention in a municipal agency: a conceptual case history. *Journal of Applied Behavioral Science,* 318–40.

Gouldner, A. W. (1954a) *Patterns of industrial bureaucracy.* New York, Free Press.

Gouldner, A. W. (1954b) *Wildcat strike.* Yellow Springs.

Gross, N., Mason, W. S., McEachern, A. W. (1957) *Explorations in role analysis: studies of the school superintendency role.* New York, Wiley.

Grove, A. S. (1983) *High output management.* New York, Random House.

Grusky, O. (1959) Role conflict in organizations: A study of prison camp officials. *Administrative Science Quarterly.*

Gunsteren, H. R. (1979) Complexiteit en cybernetische revolutie. *M & O, Tijdschrift voor organisatiekunde en sociaal beleid,* 324–39.

Halbertsma, K. T. A. (1977) Openingsrede 'Dies 1977', Stichting Interacademische Opleiding Organisatiekunde. *M & O, Tijdschrift voor organisatiekunde en sociaal beleid,* 208–11.

Harrison, R. (1971) Role negotiation: A tough minded approach to team development. In: Burke, W. W., Hornstein, H. A., *The social technology of organisation development.* Washington D.C., NTL Learning Resources Corporation.

Hart, H. W. C. van der (1983) *Leveren zonder prijssignaal*. Helmond, Wibro.

Hartman, G. J. C. (1980) Advieswerk bij interorganisationele samenwerking: een lotgeval ter lering. *M & O, Tijdschrift voor organisatiekunde en sociaal beleid*, 342–55.

Havelock, R. G., et al. (1969) *Planning for innovation*. Ann Arbor, Univ. of Mich. Institute for Social Research.

Hickson, D. J., Hinings, C. J., et al. (1971) A strategic contingency's theory of intraorganizational power. *Administrative Science Quarterly*, 216–29.

Himmelman, G. (1971) *Lohnbildung durch Kollektivverhandlungen*. Berlin, Duncker & Humblot.

Huse, E. F. (1980) *Organization development and change*. St. Paul, West Publ.

Jansen van Galen, J., van Empel, F. (1985) *Captains of industry: De economie van het ondernemen*. De Viergang.

Johnson, D. W. (1967) The use of role reversal in intergroup competition. *Journal of Personality and Social Psychology*, 135–41.

Johnson, D. W. (1972) *Reaching out: interpersonal effectiveness and selfactualization*. Engelwood Cliffs, Prentice-Hall.

Johnson, D. W., Dustin, R. (1970) The initiation of cooperation through role reversal: *Journal of Social Psychology*, 193–203.

Johnston, R., Lawrence, P. R. (1988) Beyond vertical integration: the rise of the value-adding partnership. *Harvard Business Review*, 94–101.

Judkins, Ph., West, D. (1986) *Networking in organizations. The Rank Xerox experiment*. Aldershot, Gower.

Kanter, R. M. (1983) *The change masters*. Simon & Schuster, New York.

Karras, L. L. (1974) *Give & take. The complete guide to negotiating strategies and tactics*. New York, Thomas Crowell.

Katz, F. E. (1964) The school as a complex organization. *Harvard Educational Review*.

Kepner, C. H., Tregoe, B. B. (1965) *The rational manager: A systematic approach to problem solving and decision making*. New York, McGraw-Hill.

Kilmann, R. H. (1984) *Beyond the quick fix*. Jossey-Bass, London.

Kilmann, R. H., Saxton, M. J., et al. (1985) *Gaining control of the corporate culture*. Jossey-Bass, London.

Kipnis, D. (1972) Does power corrupt? *Journal of Personality and Social Psychology*.

Koopman, M. (1975) *Macht, hoe komt u eraan, wat doet u ermee. Regels van het spel om de macht*. Baarn, Meulenhoff.

Korda, M. (1975) *Macht, hoe komt u eraan, wat doet u ermee. Regels van het spel om de macht*. Baarn, Meulenhoff.

Kotter, J. P. (1979) *Power in management*. New York, Amacon.

Lakin, M. (1972) *Interpersonal encounter: Theory and conflict in sensitivity training*, hfdst, 9: Training and conflict amelioration. New York, McGraw-Hill, 237–77.

Lammers, C. J. (1974) *Ontwikkeling en relevantie van de organisatie sociologie*. Leiden, Sociologisch Instituut.

Lammers, C. J. (1983) *Organisaties vergelijkenderwijs*. Het Spectrum, Utrecht.

Landsberger, H. A. (1961) The horizontal dimension in a bureaucracy. *Administrative Science Quarterly*.

Lawrence, P. R., Lorsch, J. W. (1967) *Organization and environment: managing differentiation and integration*. Homewood, Ill., Irwin.

Levi, A. M., Benjamin, A. (1977) Focus and flexibility in a model of conflict resolution. *Journal of Conflict Resolution*, 405–25.

Likert, R. (1961) *New patterns of management*. New York, McGraw-Hill.

Lincoln, J. A., Miller, J. (1979) Work and friendship ties in organizations: A comparative analysis of relational networks. *Administrative Science Quarterly*, 181–200.

Luscuere, C. (1979) Het ontwerpen van organisaties. *M & O, Tijdschrift voor organisatiekun de en sociaal beleid*, 350–358.

Maier, N. R. F. (1963) *Problem-solving discussions and conferences*. New York, McGraw-Hill.

March, J. G., Simon, H. A. (1958) *Organizations*. New York, Wiley.

Margerison, C., Leary, M. (1975) Managing industrial conflicts. *Management Decision*, 195–288.

Marx, E. C. H. (1971) Personeelbeleid en organisatieverandering. *M & O, Tijdschrift voor organisatiekunde en sociaal beleid*. 93–107.

Marx, E. C. H. (1975) *De organisatie van scholengemeenschappen in onderwijskundige optiek*. Groningen, Tjeenk Willink.

Marx, E. C. H. (1978) De organisatie-adviseur als procesbegeleider. *Maandblad voor Accountancy en Bedrijfshuishoudkunde*, 387–96.

Mastenbroek, W. F. G. (1977) Conflicthantering en onderhandelen. *Intermediair*, 5.

Mastenbroek, W. F. G. (1979a) Conflicthantering: een procesbenadering. *M & O, Tijdschrift voor organisatiekunde en sociaal beleid*, 69–89.

Mastenbroek, W. F. G. (1980a) Onderhandelen. *Handboek managementmethoden en-technie ken*. Deventer, Kluwer.

Mastenbroek, W. F. G. (1980b) Negotiating: A conceptual model. *Group & Organization Studies*, 324–40.

Mastenbroek, W. F. G. (1982) *Conflicthantering en organisatie-ontwikkeling*. Alphen aan den Rijn, Samsom. 1st edn.

Mastenbroek, W. F. G. (1984) Excellente organisaties: Partijen of systemen. *M & O, Tijdschrift voor organisatiekunde en sociaal beleid*.

McGregor, D. (1960) *The human side of enterprise*. New York, McGraw-Hill.

Meyer, M. W. (1972) *Bureaucratic structure and authority*. New York, Harper and Row.

Michels, R. (1970) *Zur soziologie des Parteiwesens in der modernen Demokratie*. Stuttgart.

Miles, R. E. (1989) Adapting to technology and competition, *California Management Review*, Winter.

Miles, R. E., Snow, L. L. (1986) Organizations: new concepts for new forms. *California Management Review*, Spring, **28**(8), 62–73.

Miller, D. C. (1967) Supervisor: Evolution of an organizational role. In: Bell, G. D. (ed.), *Organizations and human behaviour*. Englewood Cliffs, Prentice-Hall.

Miller, L. M. (1985) *Naar een nieuwe ondernemingscultuur*. Veen, Utrecht.

Mintzberg, H. (1979) *The structuring of organizations*. Englewood Cliffs, New Jersey, Prentice Hall.

Mintzberg, H., Raisinghani, D., Théorêt, A. (1976) The structure of unstructured decision processes. *Administrative Science Quarterly*, 246–75.

Moore, W. (1947) *Industrial relations and the social order*. New York, Macmillan.

Morris, W. C., Sashkin, M. (1976) *Organization behavior in action*. St. Paul, West Publishing Co.

Mulder, M. (1977) *Omgaan met macht*. Amsterdam, Agon Elsevier.

Nijkerk, K. J. (1981) De laboratoriummethode van training in Nederland, ontwikkelingen en dilemma's. In: Huijg, J. P. *et al.* (eds.), *Leren en leven met groepen*. Alphen aan den Rijn, Samsom.

Nijkerk, K. J., (ed.) (1975) *Training in tussenmenselijke verhoudingen*. Alphen, Samsom.

Oost, P. van (1978) De laboratoriummethode voor leren; geschiedenis van het NTL. In: Huijg, J. P. *et al.* (eds), *Leren en leven met groepen*. Alphen aan den Rijn, Samsom.

Ouchi, W. G. (1981) *Theory Z*. Addison-Wesley.

Pascale, A. T., Athos, A. G. (1981) *The art of Japanese management*. New York, Simon & Schuster.

Peters, T. J., Waterman, R. H. (1982) *In search of excellence*. New York, Harper & Row.

Peters, T. J., Austin, N. (1985) *A passion for excellence*. New York, Random House.

Pettigrew, A. M. (1973) *The politics of organizational decision-making*. London, Tavistock.

Pettigrew, A. M. (1975) Towards a political theory of organizational intervention. *Human Relations*, 191–208.

Pfeffer, J. (1978) *Organizational design*. Arlington Heights, Ill., AHM Publishing Corporation.

Pinchott, G., III (1986) *Intrapreneuring: Why You Don't Have to Leave the Corporation to Become an Entrepreneur*. New York, Harper & Row.

Pondy, L. R. (1967) Organizational conflict: Concepts and methods. *Administrative Science Quarterly*, 296–320.

Praag, W. E. van (1981) Het failliet van de human relationsbeweging in de methode van persoonlijke interventie. In: Huyg, J. P. *et al.* (eds.), *Leren en leven met groepen*. Alphen aan den Rijn, Samsom.

Rice, A. K. (1970) *The modern university: A model organization*.

Ritzer, G. (1972) *Man and his work: Conflict and change*. Englewood Cliffs, Prentice-Hall.

Robbins, S. P. (1974) *Managing organizational conflict: A nontraditional approach*. Englewood Cliffs, Prentice-Hall.

Roethlisberger, F. J. (1944) The foreman: Master and victim of double talk. *Harvard Business Review*, 283–98.

Roethlisberger, F. J., Dickson, W. J. (1939) *Management and the worker*. Cambridge, Mass., Harvard University Press.

Rubin, J. L., Brown, B. R. (1975) *The social psychology of bargaining and negotiation*. New York, Academic Press.

Rubinstein, M. (1977) Macht in adviesprocessen. In: Bunt, A. W. J. E. *et al.* (ed.), *Macht in en rond organisaties*. Alphen aan den Rijn, Samsom.

Schein, E. H. (1969) *Process consultation: its role in organization development*. Reading, Mass., Addison-Wesley.

Schein, E. H. (1985) *Organizational culture and leadership*. Jossey-Bass, London.

Schumpeter, J. A. (1954) *Capitalism, socialism and democracy*, 4th edn. London, George Allen & Unwin.

Scheiss, E. H. and Bennis, ?. (1965) ????

Schutz, W. C. (1973) *Allemaal*. The Hague, Bert Bakker.

Scott, W. F. (1981) *The skills of negotiating*. Hampshire, Gower.

Sherif, M. (1966) *In common predicament*. Boston, Houghton Mifflin.

Shull, F. A., Delbecq, A. L., Cummings, L. L. (1970) *Organizational decisionmaking*. New York, McGraw-Hill.

Simmons, R. G. (1957) The role of the first-line supervisor. In: Evan, W. M. (ed.), *Organizational experiments: laboratory and field research*. New York, Wiley.

Simon, H. A. (1957) *Models of man*. New York.

Simon, H. A. (1960) *The new science of management decision*. New York.

Swingle, P. G. (1976) *The management of power*. Hillsdale, Lawrence Erlbaum.

Sykes, G. M. (1956) The corruption of authority and rehabilitation. *Social Forces*.

Taylor, F. W. (1947) *Scientific management*. New York.

Tetrode, L. F. A. van (1974) *Trends in organisatie-ontwikkeling*. Delft, Universiteits Pers.

Thompson, J. D. (1960) Organizational management of conflict. *Administrative Science Quarterly*.

Thompson, J. D. (1964) Decision making, the firm and the market. In: Cooper, W. W., Leavitt, H. J., Shelly, M. W. (eds.), *New perspectives in organizational research*. New York, Wiley.

Thompson, J. D., Tuden, A. (1959) Strategies, structures and processes of organizational decision. In: Thompson, J. D., Hammond, P. B. *et al.* (eds.), *Comparative studies in administration*. Pittsburgh, Pittsburgh University Press.

Thompson, J. D. (1967) *Organizations in action*. New York, McGraw-Hill.

Torczyner, J. (1972) The political context of social change: A case study of innovation in adversity in Jerusalem. *Journal of Applied Behavioral Science*, 287–317.

Ulrich, D. N. *et al.* (1950) *Management behavior and foreman attitude*. Boston, Harvard Business School, Division of Research.

Veblen, T. (1899) *The theory of the leisure class*. New York, Macmillan.

Veen, P. (1979) *Macht slijt*. Groningen, Copygmiek Offset.

Veeren, H. (1978) Influences of traditions in problem-typification on participative decision-making. *Anglo-Dutch conference on occupational psychology*. Cambridge.

Vliert, E. van de (1969) Een nieuw diagram voor de organisatie-adviseur. *Intermediair*.

Vliert, E. van de (1977) Rolconflicten in het bedrijf. *Doelmatig bedrijfsbeheer*.

Vliert, E. van de (1978) Een overzicht van praktijktheorieën over organisatieontwikkeling. In: Huijg, J. P. *et al.* (eds.), *Leren en leven met groepen*. Alphen aan den Rijn, Samsom.

Vliert, E. van de (1980) Conflict en conflicthantering. In: Drenth, P. J. D. *et al.* (eds.), *Handboek arbeids- en organisatiepsychologie*. Deventer, Van Loghum Slaterus.

Vliert, E. van de (1981a) Het preventie-escalatiemodel van conflictinterventie. *M & O: Tijdschrift voor organisatiekunde sociaal beleid*, 332–48.

Vliert, E. van de (1981b) Hoe organisatieadviseurs reageren op hun rolconflict tussen adviseren en controleren. In: Bunt, P. A. E. van de (ed.), *Handboek organisatie*. Alphen aan den Rijn, Samsom.

Vliet, G. E. van (1979) *Bedrijvenwerk als vorm van belangenbehartiging*. Alphen aan den Rijn, Samsom.

Vlist, R. van der (1981) *De dynamiek van sociale systemen*. Alphen aan den Rijn, Samsom.

Vrakking, W. J. (1985) Ontwerpen via cultuurinterventies. *M & O, Tijdschrift voor organisatiekunde en sociaal beleid*.

Vucht Tijssen, J. van, Broecke, A. A. J. van de, Dijkhuizen, N. van, Reiche H. M. J. K. I., Wolff, Ch. J. de (1978) *Middenkader en stress*. The Hague COP/SER.

Walker, Ch. R. *et al.* (1956) *The foreman on the assembly line*. Cambridge, Mass., Harvard University Press.

Walton, R. E. (1965) Two strategies of social change and their dilemma's. *Journal of Applied Behavioral Science*, 167–79.

Walton, R. E. (1969) *Interpersonal peacemaking: confrontations and third party consultation*. Reading, Mass., Addison-Wesley.

Walton, R. E. (1970) A problem-solving workshop on border conflicts in Eastern Africa. *Journal of Applied Behavioral Science*, 453–89.

Walton, R. E. (1972) Interorganizational decision making and identity conflict. In:

Tuite, M., Chisholm, R., Radnor, M. (eds.), *Interorganizational decision making*. Chicago, Aldine Publishing Co.

Walton, R. E., Dutton, J. M., Cafferty, T. P. (1969) Organizational context and interdepartmental conflict. *Administrative Science Quarterly*, 73–84.

Walton, R. E., McKersie, R. B. (1965) *A behavioral theory of labor negotiations*. New York, McGraw-Hill.

White, H. (1961) Management conflict and sociometric structure. *American Journal of Sociology*, 185–99.

Wildavsky, A. (1964) *The politics of the budgetary process*. Boston, Little, Brown.

Wray, D. E. (1949) Marginal men of industry: the foreman. *American Journal of Sociology*.

Wrapp, H. E. (1984) Good managers don't make policy decisions. *Harvard Business Review*.

Zaleznik, A., Kets de Vries, M. F. (1975) *Power and the corporate mind*. Boston, Houghton Mifflin.

Zaltman, G. and Duncan, R. (1977) *Strategies for planned change*. New York, Wiley.

Zartman, W., Bermann, M. R. (1982) *The practical negotiator*. New Haven, Yale University Press.

Zwart, L. J. (1972) *Gericht veranderen van organisaties: beheerste ontwikkeling als permanente aktiviteit*. Rotterdam, Lemniscaat.

Author Index

Subject Index